COUNTRY INNS
OF THE FAR WEST

COUNTRY INNS
OF THE FAR WEST

JACQUELINE KILLEEN
CHARLES C. MILLER
California

RACHEL BARD
PETER and NEVA VOGEL
Pacific Northwest

ROY KILLEEN
Illustrations

101 PRODUCTIONS
San Francisco

Maps designed and executed by Lynne Parode.

Drawings on pages 16, 107 and 110 courtesy of inns.

Second Printing, November, 1977

Printed and bound in the United States of America.

Distributed to the book trade in the United States
by Charles Scribner's Sons, New York and in Canada
by Van Nostrand Reinhold Ltd., Toronto

Published by 101 Productions
834 Mission Street
San Francisco, California 94103

Library of Congress Cataloging in Publication Data

Main entry under title:

Country inns of the Far West.

    Includes index.
    1. Hotels, taverns, etc.—The West—Directories.
2. Hotels, taverns, etc.—British Columbia—
Directories. I. Killeen, Jacqueline.
TX907.C68   647'.9479   77-10015
ISBN 0-89286-120-7

CONTENTS

INTRODUCTION

A "country inn" is not a matter of geography. "Country" is an intangible location, bespeaking a state of mind, a refuge of tranquility, which could be found in an urban as well as a pastoral environment. "Country" inns can and do exist in cities.

Most dictionaries define an "inn" in prosaic terms as a public house which provides food and lodging. But a country inn in our sense of the word provides much more than an answer to hunger and fatigue. A visit to one of these inns may be a journey to the past. It may be your escape from pressure, from the humdrum weekly routine. Or it may be a comfortable sojourn in a spot set amid some of our nation's most spectacular scenic areas. Or your headquarters for outdoor adventure and recreation. Or just a place where you will be well fed and well treated and can sit in the garden and breathe fresh air.

One thing we can promise you: The country inns in this book are not stereotyped. The only thing they have in common is a commitment to quality, individuality and friendliness. Otherwise each goes its own way—which is definitely not the way of the standardized, computerized motels and hotels that dominate most of our travel guidebooks. And that, basically, is why we come to them: for a different experience. Looking for a change, a refreshment in our lives, we happily relinquish our king-size beds to cuddle in an old-fashioned four-poster. On arising we prefer the sound of the Pacific surf or the wind in the pines or the baaing of sheep to the morning news on television. We'll patiently wait our turn in the community bathroom because time no longer matters. We'll be glad to join our fellow guests for a family-style dinner at a long wood table.

This is not to say that the inns in this book are lacking in creature comforts. True, some are rustic and simple and may date back to the turn of the century. But many do have television, even color television, telephones, elegant dining rooms, king-size beds and a modern tiled bath for each room. And all, even the recently constructed ones, demonstrate a proper regard for the best traditions of innkeeping.

RULES OF THE INN

Reservations, Deposits and Rates Reservations are advised for all of the inns in this book, especially during peak travel periods. On holidays and weekends, they are often booked for months in advance. Most of the inns require a deposit of at least one night's lodging; call or write in advance and ask about the current requirement. Rates quoted in this book were in effect at the time of publication and are subject to change at any time.

Housekeeping In many of the smaller inns, guests share a community bathroom. Be sure to clean out your tub and wash basin, pick up your towels and leave the bathroom in immaculate condition for the next guest. In many of these small places, the chambermaid is actually the innkeeper; keep your room as tidy as possible.

Tipping In the larger inns, where you are presented your check at the end of each meal, tip as you would in any hotel or restaurant. In the smaller inns, where the owner does the cooking and serving, you are not required to tip. In fact most will not accept tips and some would be insulted. If you wish to express your appreciation, send flowers or leave a bottle of wine as you would in a friend's home. You should, however, compensate the innkeeper's helpers. Some inns have a "kitty" and divide the tips among the workers; others expect you to tip individually. We recommend that, at the end of your stay, you ask the innkeeper for advice in handling this.

CALIFORNIA MISSION COUNTRY

Santa Barbara
Along the Big Sur
To Monterey

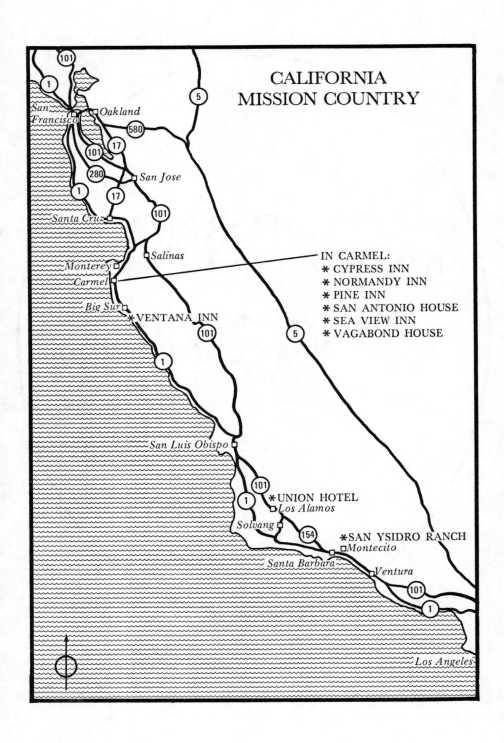

CALIFORNIA
MISSION COUNTRY

101
1
San Francisco
Oakland
580
17
101
280
San Jose
1
17
101
Santa Cruz
Salinas
Monterey
Carmel
Big Sur
VENTANA INN
101
1

5
5

IN CARMEL:
* CYPRESS INN
* NORMANDY INN
* PINE INN
* SAN ANTONIO HOUSE
* SEA VIEW INN
* VAGABOND HOUSE

San Luis Obispo
101
1
UNION HOTEL
Los Alamos
Solvang
154
SAN YSIDRO RANCH
Montecito
Santa Barbara
Ventura
101
1
Los Angeles

SAN YSIDRO RANCH
Montecito

The first innkeepers in the West were the Spanish padres who came to California in 1769 and built a string of 21 missions from San Diego to Sonoma. The missions were spaced a day's journey apart, so that travelers could find food and lodging each night. These Franciscan fathers were also the West's first ranchers, farmers and winemakers. Herds of cattle grazed on land around their outposts and from their orchards, gardens and vineyards came an abundance of food for the mission tables.

In 1786 the padres founded their tenth mission at the base of the Santa Ynez Mountains, which rise from the bay at Santa Barbara. After the 1812 earthquake, the mission was rebuilt and became known as Queen of the Missions for the beauty of its Moorish-Spanish architecture and the affluence of the surrounding rancheros.

Among the holdings of the Santa Barbara padres was San Ysidro, a citrus and cattle ranch high in the Santa Ynez Mountains with views of the oak-studded hills sloping to the Pacific far below. After the missions were secularized, new owners built rustic stone and wooden cottages among the groves of orange trees, eucalypti and palms. By 1893, San Ysidro had become a guest ranch. The old adobe, built by the Franciscans in 1825, still stands. And guests dine today in a stone building, once used as a citrus packing house.

San Ysidro's most illustrious era was in the 1930s and 1940s when Ronald Colman and State Senator Alvin Weingand jointly owned the

11

ranch. The guest book from those years reads like a combination of *Burke's Peerage* and *Who's Who* in politics, literature and show business. Sir Winston Churchill wrote part of his memoirs in a house shaded by a large magnolia tree. Somerset Maugham produced several short stories in a cottage banked by geraniums. John Galsworthy sought seclusion here to work on the *Forsyte Saga*. David Niven, Merle Oberon and Rex Harrison found life at the ranch a respite from the glitter of Hollywood. Laurence Olivier and Vivien Leigh were married in the gardens. And later John F. Kennedy brought his bride to San Ysidro for their honeymoon in an ivy-covered stone cottage.

After Colman and Weingand, San Ysidro had a succession of owners. Through years of neglect, its facilities degenerated along with its reputation. The ranch was in deplorable condition by 1976 when it was rescued by Jim Lavenson, former president of the Plaza Hotel in New York City.

After searching over a year for a hotel of his own, Lavenson had come west to bid on the Santa Barbara Biltmore, but ended up buying San Ysidro instead. "Everyone thought I was crazy and so did I. The buildings hadn't been painted for 15 years," he guesses. Hardly a plant or a blade of grass was still alive. "There was one lawn mower and one vacuum cleaner and neither worked."

Lavenson and his wife, Susie, packed up their 13 rooms of furnishings and moved west. In less than a year most of the cottages were gleaming with fresh white paint outside. Susie charmingly furnished them with her own antiques interspersed with bargains culled from sales and the Salvation Army. "Susie talks about doing it on a shoestring," Jim Lavenson laughs. "Then she'll hang a $5,000 mirror next to a $5 rocking chair."

Most of the cottages contain living room and bedroom, often with wood-burning fireplaces in each. Many have enclosed porches with views of the ocean or the wooded creek which runs through the property. Susie has splashed the rooms with color: bright upholstery and carpets, flowery quilted bedspreads, prints and paintings, bowls of fresh flowers, books. And the Lavensons say "welcome" in a very personal way: Each arriving guest finds his own name etched on a shingle by his cottage door.

Another custom instigated by Lavenson is the "honor bar." At a well-stocked table in the lounge of the main hacienda, guests mix their own drinks and write up their own chits. Among other comforts of the

San Ysidro Ranch

lounge is a large stone fireplace, a piano, game tables and a chessboard. Next door the dining room serves three meals a day from hearty breakfasts (juice from freshly squeezed oranges, often from the ranch's own trees) to candlelit dinners prepared by a French chef. The Lavensons have furnished the stone-walled room with many of their own family heirlooms, including a hutch which belonged to Jim's great-grandmother and now displays a set of pewter cups from the Plaza Hotel, a gift on his resignation.

Today San Ysidro's lovely gardens are abloom with marigolds, daisies, roses and geraniums, and the orchards are again bearing fruit. Lavenson has rebuilt the stables to shelter the fine quarter horses and Arabians which guests may ride over 500 miles of mountain trails. The tennis court has been resurfaced. The swimming pool is surrounded by gardens and neatly tended lawns. And for evening entertainment, there's an excellent combo in the stone cellar of the dining house.

If all this is not enough to keep one amused at San Ysidro Ranch, the city of Santa Barbara is only minutes away. There are splendid beaches here and sportfishing, too. Among the better restaurants, one may find French food at La Grange, seafood and Spanish dishes at Casa Sevilla, and unhurried elegance with an ocean view at the Biltmore, one of the last of the grand hotels. The Santa Barbara Museum of Art houses a number of interesting collections. And a visit to the mission, one of the most beautiful and well preserved in the state, recalls the days when the Spanish padres were this city's only innkeepers.

SAN YSIDRO RANCH, 900 San Ysidro Lane, Montecito, California 93108. Telephone: (805) 969-5046. Accommodations: twin, double and king-size beds; private baths with tub/shower; telephones in all rooms; no television. Rates: from $39 double, suites from $78; no meals included; $3 daily charged for dogs; horses boarded for $12 daily. Children welcome. Cards: AE, BA, MC. Open all year.

Getting There: From San Francisco or Los Angeles take Highway 101 to Santa Barbara; just south of the city in Montecito, take San Ysidro Road east through Montecito Village to San Ysidro Lane. From San Francisco or Los Angeles, Santa Barbara may be reached by rail via Amtrak and by air via United Airlines. Hughes Airwest and Apollo Airways also fly here from San Francisco and Golden West from Los Angeles.

UNION HOTEL
Los Alamos

A year after founding Santa Barbara Mission, the Spanish padres moved north and in 1787 established Mission La Purisima Concepción, which became the seat of mission government in California from 1815 to 1823. In 1803 the Franciscans founded Mission Santa Inez, where the Danish community of Solvang now flourishes. Between the two missions, in a long fertile valley, is the township of Los Alamos. This agricultural town, however, did not come into being until 1876. Four years later a wooden hotel was built here to lodge passengers from the Wells Fargo stagecoaches. After a fire, the hotel was rebuilt of adobe; then the highway and history bypassed Los Alamos and the hotel was boarded up. Recent owners attempted to modernize it in the 1960s and removed whatever traces of antiquity were left.

In 1972, Dick Langdon, a Los Angeles meat wholesaler seeking a new way of life, bought the old hotel and vowed to restore it in 1880 style. With the help of Jim Radhe, a talented young craftsman, Langdon dismantled 12 old barns and rebuilt the facade of the hotel exactly as it appeared in an 1884 photograph. Inside they stripped decades of paint to reveal the original woodwork and brass. Rooms were papered with colorful Victorian prints.

Langdon spent a year touring the United States to find antiques. In the high-ceilinged downstairs parlor, a pair of 200-year-old Egyptian burial urns and hand-carved chairs from Alabama flank an intricately chiseled fireplace mantel from a mansion in Pasadena. A coffee table has been constructed from an oak-framed copper bathtub. There's an 1885 Singer sewing machine, chandeliers from Lee J. Cobb's home and the hotel's original safe, blackened on one side from an early shooting. Swinging doors, from a bordello in New Orleans, lead into a saloon with a 150-year-old bar of solid African mahogany.

The large dining room contains furnishings and gaslights from a plantation in Mississippi. Tables are set with lace cloths and an array of old chinaware, no two dishes quite alike. Langdon's girlfriend, Teri Zibrida, cooks big family-style dinners, prepared from recipes she found in *The Home Queen Cookbook*, published in the 19th century. There are tureens of minestrone, cornbread with honey butter, platters of beef and Southern-fried chicken, bowls of fresh vegetables and, for dessert, strawberry fritters. If he's in the mood, Dick turns off the lights

Union Hotel

after dinner and plays his tapes of *The Shadow, Inner Sanctum* and other old-time radio thrillers.

Upstairs are 14 bedrooms and a second parlor with a Brunswick pool table inlaid with ivory. Some of the beds could be museum pieces. One room houses a two-centuries-old Australian brass and cast-iron bedstead with insets of cloisonné. In another there is an original Murphy bed, concealed in a mahogany armoire. Vintage patchwork quilts and crocheted spreads serve as covers, and even the bedside Bibles are circa 1880. Langdon designates his rooms as dry rooms (sharing a common bath) and wet rooms (private bath). In these he has installed overhead wooden water tanks and replaced the linoleum flooring with hexagonal tiles.

"There is really nothing to do here," Langdon warns. "You live as they lived 100 years ago. Nobody is going to entertain you and if you can't live with yourself, you shouldn't come here." Los Alamos, however, does have an excellent antique shop and old-fashioned general store and there is horseback riding and a lake nearby. Solvang and the missions can be explored. And there are two outstanding restaurants in the area—the Danish Inn and the Ballard Store.

When Dick Langdon completes his master plan for the hotel, however, there will be more than enough to do here. In the yard he intends to create an 1880s park with a croquet course, clay tennis court, horseshoe pits, and a swimming hole. Then one day he hopes to have a fleet of 1900-vintage cars to take his guests sightseeing. And eventually a wardrobe department so visitors to the hotel can dress up in Victorian attire. "I'll never be finished," he confesses eagerly. "I have a lifetime of work ahead of me. But I'm not doing this for money. I'm doing it for love."

UNION HOTEL, 362 Bell Street, Los Alamos, California 93440. Telephone: dial operator and ask for Los Alamos 2744 in area code 805. Accommodations: twin and double beds; some private baths with tub/shower, community bathrooms with tubs and showers; no television; no telephones. Rates: $25 for "dry" rooms, $35 for "wet" rooms, continental breakfast included. Meal Service: dinner only; full bar service. No children. No pets. No credit cards. Open all year, Friday, Saturday and Sunday only.

VENTANA INN
Big Sur

Between San Simeon, where Hearst built his castle, and Monterey, the Santa Lucia Mountains rise precipitously above the incessantly pounding Pacific surf. Today Highway 1 traverses this rugged terrain across high bridges and along niches blasted out of the cliffs. The Spanish missionaries found this section of the coast impassable and detoured inland. But this very remoteness appealed to one of the first settlers, a Yankee sea captain with the unlikely name of Juan Bautista Roger Cooper who landed his cargoes at the mouth of Big Sur River to avoid paying customs duties to the Mexicans in Monterey. The struggles of the homesteaders who later tried to farm this land inspired the poetry of Robinson Jeffers.

But it was another writer who shaped the destiny of Big Sur. Henry Miller moved here in 1944, seeking the serenity of the coastal mountains after his expatriate days in Paris. Other artists followed, many moving into the abandoned shacks of the convicts who had constructed the bridges for the coastal highway. For the next decade or so Big Sur was a Bohemian community of hard-working artists.

Only recently has the traveler to Big Sur been able to sleep in style. In 1975, the Ventana Inn was built on a meadow 1,200 feet above the Pacific. The contemporary architecture is almost as spectacular as the Big Sur itself, with soaring ceilings, giant beams, unexpected angles and planes. From every room there are views of the mountains, the meadow or the ocean far below. The rooms are paneled with knotty pine and handsomely appointed with wicker furniture, hand-painted headboards and patchwork quilts from Nova Scotia. Some have Franklin stoves, or window seats tucked in alcoves. All have private balconies or patios and luxurious carpeted baths. There are also some two-story units with kitchenettes and living rooms.

A fire in the lobby helps remove the chill from the morning fogs which often shroud the Santa Lucia range. Here guests receive a light breakfast—bowls of fruit compote, croissants, date and nut breads and coffee. Across the meadow on another hilltop is the Ventana's restaurant which offers a diverse selection of lunch and dinner dishes. One word of caution: In the inn's short history, chefs have come and gone, and the cooking has varied from outstanding to less-than-satisfactory, although the setting almost compensates for the food.

There is a large swimming pool at the Ventana Inn, a sauna and a Jacuzzi. And there are hiking trails in the mountains above. Down the road is Nepenthe, a restaurant and bar of intriguing design, built around a cabin which Orson Welles once bought for Rita Hayworth (although they never lived there). Nepenthe was the gathering place for Henry Miller's followers. Today on a sunny afternoon the broad deck is crowded with locals and visitors sipping wine or beer, while enjoying the recorded classical music and a breathtaking view of the coast.

Ventana is only an hour or so by car from La Casa Grande, the Spanish-style castle built by William Randolph Hearst for Marion Davies in the 1920s. Located on a hilltop above the small port of San Simeon, Hearst Castle is now owned by the State of California, which conducts daily tours through the grandiose rooms. Tickets for a castle tour should be reserved well in advance. Tour reservations and information are handled by Ticketron, Inc., 427 Merchant Street, San Francisco, California 94903.

VENTANA INN, Big Sur, California 93920. Telephone: (408) 667-2331. Accommodations: queen-size beds or twin queens; private baths with tub/shower; television; telephones. Rates: $52-$87 double, $10 for each additional person in room, townhouse suites $140 for up to four persons, no additional charge for children under 11, continental breakfast included. Meal Service: lunch and dinner; full bar service. Children welcome. No pets. Cards: AE, BA, MC. Open all year.

Getting There: From San Francisco, follow directions to Monterey and take Highway 1 south. From Los Angeles, take Highway 101 to San Luis Obispo and Highway 1 north.

MONTEREY PENINSULA

In 1770 the Franciscan padres, led by Junipero Serra, founded Mission San Carlos in Monterey, the second in California's chain of missions. A year later, Father Serra moved the mission to Carmel, and later returned here to spend his last years. The Spanish military expedition which Serra accompanied had established a presidio in Monterey. In 1775 Spain designated Monterey as the capital of California and so it remained through the Mexican rule until the American flag was raised over the Customhouse in 1846.

Monterey had become a cultivated town, where the Spanish citizens and their families lived auspiciously in two-story adobe casas with roofs of red tile. Then the Yankees discovered the abundance of whales offshore and turned this sedate Spanish community into a bustling whaling port. Sardine fishing brought added prosperity; west of town, Cannery Row was built and later immortalized in the works of John Steinbeck. Today many of the old adobes are open to the public or house restaurants and shops. And after the sardines had all but disappeared, Cannery Row was converted into a complex of shops and dining places.

Steinbeck was not the only writer beguiled by this lovely peninsula. Robert Louis Stevenson lived in Monterey in 1879. Then after the turn of the century a group of writers and artists settled in Carmel. Edward Weston, Maynard Dixon, Ambrose Bierce, Don Blanding, Lincoln Steffens and Robinson Jeffers lived here over the years. Today there are 66 art galleries within the village itself. Although Carmel is built in a potpourri of architectural styles—from Victorian and half-timbered cottage to neo-Spanish—new construction or remodeling is strictly controlled to preserve the woodsy, village-like quality of the picturesque streets.

Few places in the West offer such diverse recreational facilities as the Monterey Peninsula. There are eight public and four private golf courses. Sailboats may be chartered in Monterey Bay. Skin diving, scuba diving, fishing, tennis, polo matches—they're all here. Then there is the spectacular shoreline to explore from the cypress-bordered white sand dunes of Carmel to the rocky coves and hidden beaches of Lovers Point. Carmel is a shopper's paradise with a plethora of crafts, jewelry, clothing and antique stores. It's a sightseer's mecca, too, whether

reliving history at the old mission or viewing the palatial mansions along Pebble Beach's famed Seventeen-Mile Drive.

The Monterey Peninsula probably has more restaurants per capita than any other area of the West. The 200 or so dining places encompass almost every ethnic cuisine. A few of the best include Raffaello in Carmel for northern Italian food, Maison Bergerac in Pacific Grove for French cooking in a restored Victorian mansion, the Whaling Station Inn near Cannery Row for fresh seafood and the atmosphere of Early California. If you're in the mood for Japanese food, there is Shabu-Shabu in Carmel, or if you want to get away from it all for a casual evening and creative cooking there is The Clock Garden in Monterey. Reservations at these restaurants for weekends should be made several days in advance.

It is surprising that among Monterey's treasure troves of history there is not an old Spanish inn. Luxury hotels, standard motels, but none that meet the criteria of an inn. On the other hand nearly all the hostelries of Carmel have some qualities of a country inn, even some of the motels. Pine Inn is the oldest and most historic, but there are a large number of smaller inns and guest houses. A few of these are described on the following pages.

Getting There: From San Francisco take Highway 101 to the Monterey Peninsula cutoff, north of Salinas; in Castroville this joins Highway 1, which goes through Monterey to Carmel. For a longer and more scenic route from San Francisco, take Highway 280 to San Jose, Highway 17 through Los Gatos to Santa Cruz, and Highway 1 south to Monterey. From Los Angeles, take Highway 101 to Salinas and Highway 68 to Monterey; or for a more scenic but much longer drive, leave Highway 101 at San Luis Obispo and take Highway 1 through Morro Bay and the Big Sur to Carmel. There are direct flights daily to Monterey Airport from Los Angeles and San Francisco via United Airlines and Hughes Airwest. Commuter Air West has flights from Lake Tahoe, San Jose and San Francisco.

PINE INN
Carmel

In 1902, the year after Queen Victoria's death, Pine Inn opened its doors bringing all the gaudiness of the Victorian era to Carmel. The town was then a quiet refuge for artists and writers. But at the turn of the century Carmel had also been discovered by land developers who built Pine Inn to house prospective purchasers of lots, which cost $250 apiece! As the land boom prospered and Carmel grew, so did Pine Inn. The old Carmelo Hotel was moved from another location to serve as an annex; new wings were added haphazardly until the inn occupied most of a block by 1960. At that time Pine Inn was purchased by the McKee family who have carefully maintained its Victorian ambience.

Pine Inn is located on Ocean Avenue, Carmel's heavily trafficked thoroughfare. Yet a step inside is a step into the past. The original building houses the lobby and a bevy of dining rooms decorated with deep red carpeting, flocked and flowered wallpapers, massive wooden sideboards, electrified gas lamps. There is also a cozy bar with stained-glass windows, marble-topped tables and a cast-iron fireplace—marvelous for a drink on a foggy day. A large brick patio was covered with a glass dome a few years back and converted into a gardenlike dining area.

The inn has 49 bedrooms of which no two are alike. Those in the older part of the inn are small, but have the most historic charm. They are decorated in *fin de siècle* style with chintz wallpapers, white shutters and wainscotings, marble-topped wooden chests and brass bedsteads. In the newer additions, the rooms are larger and the furnishings are more modern and luxurious. An ornately furnished penthouse suite with fireplace opens to a private patio and will accommodate eight.

PINE INN, Ocean Avenue, P.O. Box 250, Carmel, California 93921. Telephone: (408) 624-3890. Accommodations: twin, double and king-size beds; private baths with tub/shower; color television; telephones. Rates: $21-$38 single, $21-$48 double, $28-$50 triple, $38-$60 suites, $3 for rollaway or cot in room; no meals included. Meal Service: breakfast, lunch and dinner; full bar service. Facilities for small conferences up to 50. Children welcome. No pets. Cards: AE, BA, MC. Open all year.

Normandy Inn

NORMANDY INN
Carmel

On the south side of Ocean Avenue is a French Provincial complex of buildings designed and built by architect Robert Stanton and decorated by his wife Virginia, former party editor of *House Beautiful*. After graduating from UC Berkeley, Stanton worked for architect Wallace Neff on a number of Hollywood homes, including Douglas Fairbanks' Pickfair, and the Fredric March home, which inspired his interest in French Provincial design. Stanton moved to Carmel to practice architecture, and built the Normandy Inn in 1937. Over the years newer and larger units were added and a group of cottages were built across the street. Today the Normandy has 47 units clustered around gardens, banked with pots of blooming flowers, and a kidney-shaped pool.

The older rooms have the atmosphere of a French country inn. Many have corner fireplaces adorned with painted tiles. Multipaned windows look out to the trees and gardens, or occasionally offer a glimpse of the ocean beyond. There are shuttered alcoves and beds tucked into niches in the wall. The newer units have more luxurious appointments such as king-size beds and large picture windows, but lack some of the charm of the older rooms. The cottages across the way are centered around a brick patio; there are fireplaces and kitchenettes in most of these.

In the mornings the Normandy serves guests juice, coffee and orange muffins in a quaint country dining room filled with pots of flowers. Here Virginia Stanton has installed her fine collection of antique Quimper plates from France.

NORMANDY INN, Ocean Avenue, P.O. Box 1706, Carmel, California 93921. Telephone: (408) 624-3825. Accommodations: twin, double and king-size beds; private baths, some tub/shower, some shower only; telephones in all rooms; television in newer rooms. Rates: $25-$28 single, $28-$40 double, $28-$37 triple, continental breakfast included. No other meal service. Children welcome. No pets. No credit cards. Open all year.

SEA VIEW INN
Carmel

The Sea View has been operated as an inn since the mid-1920s, but Marshall and Diane Hydorn, the present owners, think the three-story shingled house was probably built just after the turn of the century. Two of the early innkeepers here, the Misses Olive and Pearl Stout, advertised rooms for $3 a night. Hydorn speculates that this included meals as well! Located three blocks from the ocean on a quiet residential street, the inn was obviously named for its view; however, over the years large pines have grown up around the house, allowing only a peak at the sea from the upstairs rooms today.

The inn maintains the aura of Carmel in the twenties. The board and batten walls have been painted white, and the solid, comfortable furnishings of previous owners are mixed with the Hydorn's antiques. The homey living room has a large brick fireplace, shuttered windows and an oak refectory table where the Hydorns serve a morning spread of juices, dry cereals, pastries—sometimes fruit, turnovers or quiche.

The bedrooms have a country charm. Four-posters or wicker bedsteads, quilted spreads. A burled armoire in one room, a rocker in another, marble-topped dressers here and there, interspersed with pieces of no discernable lineage. In some rooms a studio couch is cozily placed in an alcove; in others there are window seats by the dormered windows. One room is called the Bridal Room. Recently, to the Hydorn's delight, a couple who had honeymooned at Sea View returned for their 50th anniversary.

SEA VIEW INN, Camino Real at 11th, P.O. Box 4138, Carmel, California 93921. Telephone: (408) 624-8778. Accommodations: twin, double, queen-size and king-size beds; some rooms with additional studio couch; some private baths, tub/shower or shower only; some community baths, tub/shower; no telephones; no television. Rates $16-$22 single, $18-$24 double, $4 for third person in room, continental breakfast included. No other meal service. Children welcome. No pets. Cards: BA, MC. Open all year.

SAN ANTONIO HOUSE
Carmel

This three-story shingled house was built in 1907 as a private residence and during its early years served as a studio and weekend retreat for artists and writers from the San Francisco Bay Area. In the 1930s Lincoln Steffens lived next door and played host to a continuous flow of the literati of his day. In 1950, the handsome old house, set back from the street by a spacious lawn, became a guest house. In 1974 Michael Cloran, a young stockbroker from Southern California, and his wife Joan came to Carmel for a weekend, bought the old house on impulse—"we wanted to change our lifestyles"—and stayed.

The Clorans live in the main floor of the house and rent the lower floor, top floor and a cottage behind as two- and three-room units. Privacy for their guests is their main concern. Each room has its own private entrance, patio, bath, and a coffeemaker and refrigerator stocked with orange juice. San Antonio is for people who want the atmosphere of a guest house without having to socialize.

Joan has decorated the rooms with vibrant colors and her own collection of European paintings and prints. One of the most delightful suites is the "studio"—three little rooms atop the house, under a gabled roof. Black wicker and wrought-iron furniture contrasts with the white board and batten walls, bright red and white print spreads and red corduroy cushions. From multipaned windows there is a view of the ocean. Baby roses cascade over the outside stairs while Martha Washingtons and geraniums bloom around the patio. A pleasant place to absorb the sun, the sound of the surf and the smell of the pines.

SAN ANTONIO HOUSE, San Antonio between 7th and Ocean, P.O. Box 3683, Carmel, California 93921. Telephone: (408) 624-4334. Accommodations: twin beds and queen-size bed in each unit; private baths with tub/shower; no telephones, but rooms have television. Rates: $26 double, $3 each additional person, coffee and juice included. No other meal service. Children welcome. Pets allowed. No credit cards. Open all year.

VAGABOND HOUSE
Carmel

Don Blanding lived here in the 1940s, but no one is certain if his poem *Vagabond's House* was named for the inn, or if the inn was later named for the poem. Nevertheless Vagabond House is a poetic hideaway with rooms looking through treetops into a stone courtyard, massed with rhododendrons and camellias. In the center, baskets of ferns and flowering plants hang from the branches of a large oak.

Vagabond House was originally built in 1941 for efficiency apartments when Carmel's population suddenly swelled from the influx of military personnel to Fort Ord. Later it became an inn. In 1974, Patsy and Chuck Watts, a young couple from Southern California, purchased the inn after searching the state for just such a place.

The rooms are large and charmingly furnished with Early American maple, pieces of wicker, quilted bedspreads and, everywhere you look, antique pendulum clocks from the Watts' large collection. Many rooms have fireplaces and some have kitchenettes, a holdover from apartment-house days. There is a coffee pot and fresh coffee in each room so guests may brew their own any time of the day. In the mornings the Watts provide fruit juice and Danish rolls for a light breakfast in the patio—or, if you prefer, in your room. The Vagabond House does not have a common living area.

VAGABOND HOUSE, 4th and Dolores, P.O. Box 2747, Carmel, California 94921. Telephone: (408) 624-9988. Accommodations: twin double, queen-size and king-size beds; private bath, some with tub/shower, some shower only; no telephones; color television. Rates: $25-$33, $6 for third person in room, continental breakfast included. No other meal service. No children under 12. No pets. No credit cards. Open all year.

Vagabond House

CYPRESS INN
Carmel

The Spanish heritage of Carmel's missionary settlers is found in this quiet inn on a side street off Ocean Avenue. Though built in the early 1920s, the inn looks almost like a colonial mission itself, with a red-tiled roof and Spanish tower. To the right of a stately entrance hall, through an arched doorway, is a spacious living room with the look of a Mediterranean villa: white stucco walls, a high beamed ceiling, large fireplace and wrought-iron chandeliers. Doors open into a tiled courtyard filled with colorful flowers: a lovely place to enjoy your coffee and sweet rolls in the morning, but if fog prevails there is a small breakfast room on the side where ferns hang from a skylight.

The rooms are built around this secluded patio and no two are quite alike in decor or furnishings, though the Mediterranean wooden furnishings and white walls are found throughout. A few of the rooms have a view of the ocean. After many owners, Cypress Inn was acquired in 1975 by the owners of Pine Inn and is now beautifully maintained.

CYPRESS INN, Lincoln and 7th, P.O. Box Y, Carmel, California 93921. Telephone: (408) 624-3871. Accommodations: twin, queen-size and king-size beds; private baths, some tub/shower, some shower only; telephones; color television. Rates: $20-$40 double, $3 extra for cot, continental breakfast included. No other meal service. Children welcome. No pets. Cards: AE, BA, MC. Open all year.

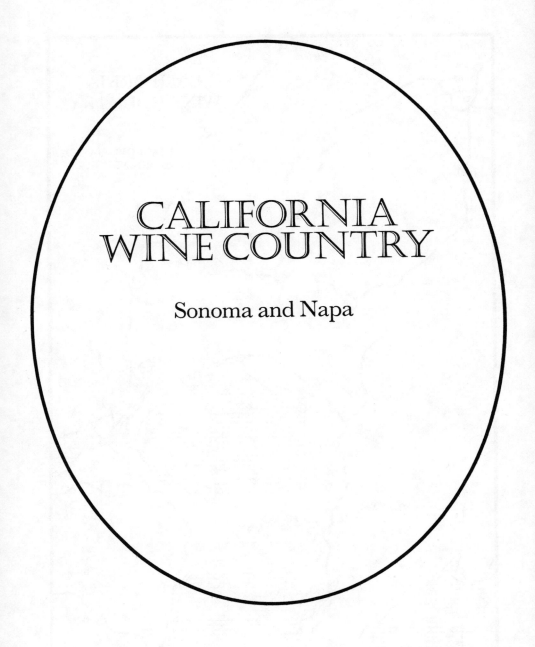

CALIFORNIA WINE COUNTRY

Sonoma and Napa

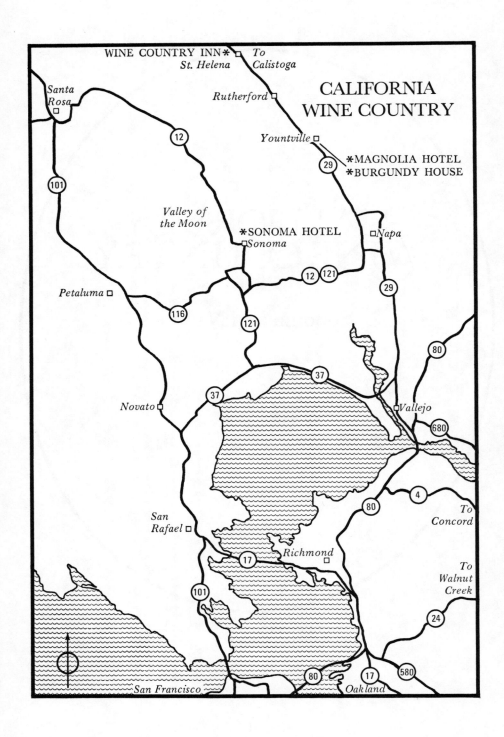

SONOMA HOTEL
Sonoma

Sonoma's large tree-shaded plaza was laid out by General Mariano Guadalupe Vallejo in 1835 when he founded Pueblo de Sonoma as Mexico's most northerly outpost against hostile Indians. Twelve years earlier Mission San Francisco Solano de Sonoma had been built there as the last northern tip of California's chain of missions. Vallejo built himself a two-story adobe *palacio* on the plaza where his regiment of Mexican soldiers marched daily. The peace was shattered on June 14, 1846, when a band of three-dozen armed Americans, acting on their own authority, captured the town, imprisoned Vallejo, and proclaimed Sonoma capital of the Bear Flag Republic. The Bear Flag flew over the Sonoma plaza until the following month, when California became part of the United States.

At the northwest corner of the plaza is the recently restored, three-story Sonoma Hotel. The tall building with its high gables was built in the 1880s to house a dry goods store on the first level and a two-story meeting hall above. About 1920 it was purchased by the winemaking Sebastiani family, who converted the cavernous hall into two floors, partitioned these into 17 rooms and rechristened it the Plaza Hotel. John and Dorene Musilli bought the hotel in 1974 and leased it to a group who ran it as the Waywith Inn. "I bought it strictly as an investment," John admits, "but Dorene has been scheming to get her hands on it ever since." When the Waywith group moved out at the end of 1976, Dorene immediately began to redecorate the hotel with antiques. "There's not one reproduction in the place."

Dorene went to see a San Francisco furniture dealer who had just received a shipment from Europe of matched French and English bedroom sets made at the turn of the century. She bought furniture for 16 rooms and almost all matches in each room—dresser, armoire, headboard, even chairs. Mattresses were custom-made to fit the odd-size beds and covered with quilted flowered spreads. Ruffled organdy curtains and a watering can full of dried flowers and weeds add a homey note to each room.

The 17th room has been named the Vallejo Room in honor of the furnishings. The monumental Italianate pieces of hand-carved burled walnut had belonged to General Vallejo's sister and are on loan to the hotel from the Sonoma League for Historic Preservation. The bed looks fit for the general himself, with an 11-foot-high backboard and a bedspread of scarlet velvet.

The Musillis stripped eight coats of paint off the wainscoting in the hotel lobby to reveal the natural dark fir and furnished the room with period pieces. A continental breakfast of juice, pastries and coffee is served here in front of a large stone fireplace.

The lower floor also contains a bar and restaurant called the Old Sonoma House. Brunch and lunch are served in a delightful flower-filled tile patio behind the hotel. A leisurely meal here, admiring the wisteria vine, magnolia trees, climbing red roses and splashing fountain, surrounded by orchids, is a lovely way to while away a sunny afternoon.

Sonoma's second important settler after General Vallejo was Colonel Agoston Haraszthy, an Hungarian nobleman who planted his Buena Vista vineyards here in the 1850s and started Northern California's winemaking industry. Sonoma has ever since been an important viticultural center. The Buena Vista's old stone cellars are open to the public. (Buy some cheese at Sonoma Cheese Company and picnic at the winery.) Tours are also conducted at the Sebastiani Winery, Hacienda Cellars, and 29 other wineries in the area.

Sonoma is rich in Californiana. The Sonoma State Historic Park maintains the mission, General Vallejo's home and the Toscano Hotel, which are open to visitors. The old barracks which has headquartered three armies—the Mexicans, the Bear Flag rebels and the Americans—is currently being restored. Near Sonoma is Valley of the Moon, last home of Jack London, now also preserved as a state park.

Sonoma Hotel

Of Sonoma's many restaurants, two are particularly outstanding. Up the street from the Sonoma Hotel is the Depot Hotel, a restored building once owned by General Vallejo; there are no overnight accommodations here but the setting is charming and the food delicious. On the road into town you will see a Victorian farmhouse which has been spruced up with redwood and art deco; this is the home of Au Relais, a delightful French restaurant.

SONOMA HOTEL, 110 West Spain Street, Sonoma, California 95476. Telephone: (707) 996-2996. Accommodations: twin and double beds; some private baths with tub, community baths with showers; no telephones; no television. Rates: $25-$40 double, continental breakfast included. Meal Service: breakfast, lunch and dinner in Old Sonoma House in lower floor of hotel; full bar service. Children welcome. No pets. Cards: AE, BA, MC. Open all year.

Getting There: From San Francisco take Highway 101 north through San Rafael to Ignacio; there take Highway 37 east to Highway 21, which leads to Sonoma.

NAPA VALLEY

This lovely long valley, caressed by gentle mountains, is one of the world's most important winemaking regions. The Franciscan fathers from nearby Sonoma Mission started making wine here in the 1820s, but it was an inferior wine made from their Mission grapes. It was not until some 30 years later, in 1858, that Charles Krug produced the first European-type wine for which the valley is now known. After Colonel Agoston Haraszthy proved that the European *vinifera* grapes would thrive north of San Francisco Bay in his Buena Vista vineyards in Sonoma, French, Italian and German immigrants flocked to the Napa Valley in the 1860s, planting cuttings from Haraszthy's stock.

This viniferous valley stretches from the town of Napa, an early timber-shipping center and once even a mining town during a silver rush in 1858, to the town of Calistoga, whose mineral spas have attracted the weary since Mormon settler Sam Brannan first discovered underground hot springs here in 1859. Towering above Calistoga is the 4,500-foot peak of Mount St. Helena, which Robert Louis Stevenson described as the "Mont Blanc of the Coast Range" after spending his honeymoon in a bunk house at the mountain's base in 1880.

One of the most interesting settlements in the valley is Yountville, named after the valley's first white settler, George Yount. In exchange for a favor to his friend, General Vallejo, the Mexican government granted Young an 11,000-acre tract of land comprising most of the Napa Valley. The old Groezinger Winery in Yountville has been converted to a fascinating complex of shops, galleries and restaurants called Vintage 1870. Next door the train depot and railroad cars house yet more shops. And along the town's picturesque streets there are antique shops, restaurants—and two country inns.

North of Yountville is Rutherford Square, where outdoor musical productions are presented in the summer months. Just north of here is St. Helena, where a museum containing Robert Louis Stevenson memorabilia is housed in a stone hatchery. Beyond the town is an old bale mill with a waterwheel 40-feet in diameter, and Freemark Abbey, another interesting complex of shops.

All through the valley, of course, are the wineries, most of which conduct tours of their cellars and tastings of their bottlings. This is unquestionably the most popular form of recreation in the valley. Space does not permit a description of all the wineries, but one stands out as spectacular over all the others. This is Sterling Vineyards, a recently built Moorish structure on a hilltop in the center of the valley between St. Helena and Calistoga. An aerial tramway whisks visitors to the winery over treetops. Inside, the winemaking operation is explained graphically, allowing visitors to tour the premises at their own pace. Afterwards, sipping wine in the late afternoons on the terrace as the mountains cast their shadows onto the vineyards below is an experience long remembered.

Other forms of recreation in the Napa Valley include aerial gliding around Calistoga, and swimming, fishing and boating at nearby manmade Lake Berryessa. The valley also offers a range of dining experiences from a very formal continental dinner at Oliver's restaurant in the city of Napa to an informal snack of homemade pâté at Bon Appétit, a French-style roadside cafe. For lunch, the Chutney Kitchen and the Vintage Cafe in Yountville are excellent, as is the Napa Cheese Company near Oakville. For lunch or dinner the Victorian and the Carriage House in Napa both offer good food in turn-of-the-century surroundings. There is luscious, freshly made pasta at Mama Nina's in Yountville.

Magnolia Hotel

Getting There: From San Francisco take Highway 101 north through San Rafael to Ignacio; there take Highway 37 east to Highway 21 north to the intersection of Highway 12 which leads east to Napa. From Napa Highway 29 extends north through Yountville, Rutherford and St. Helena to Calistoga. By air, Stol Air has flights daily from San Francisco International Airport to Napa Airport, which also accommodates private planes.

MAGNOLIA HOTEL
Yountville

This quaint three-story hotel was built in 1873 with large stones from the Silverado Trail. In its early years a traveler paid a dollar a night for a room including a barn and feed for his horse. Meals were 25 cents extra. And for those who could afford the luxury of rail travel, the hotel sent a surrey to meet them at the depot. "If these stone walls could talk, there would be some wild stories to tell," speculates the hotel's present owner Nancy Monte. She thinks the Magnolia was a brothel at one time in its checkered history and knows for sure that the cellar was raided during Prohibition for bootlegging activities.

When Nancy and her husband Ray bought the Magnolia in 1968, it long had been boarded up and was in bad condition. "We worked on it for two years while living here with our four children—it was terrible," she remembers. Today the hotel's six bedrooms are freshly painted and papered and furnished with antiques—four-poster beds, marble-topped tables with a crystal decanter of port, crocheted bedspreads. But nostalgia stops with the plumbing; all rooms have modern baths. The third floor rooms adjoin a little sitting room. "Often two couples take over the entire third floor," Nancy says.

Downstairs is a comfortable sitting room and a family dining room where Nancy serves a hearty breakfast: juice, fruit, French toast from freshly baked bread or sourdough pancakes with port-wine syrup, bacon and coffee. It's good home cooking.

Yet there's nothing "home-cooked" about the Magnolia's dinners. The Montes have acquired the services of a French chef. The dinners are served in two areas: by the fireside in a gracefully decorated former antique shop next door to the hotel, and downstairs in the "bootleggers" cellar. There is only a single entrée nightly on the prix fixe dinners which are very expensive for the area. Recently Ray and Nancy installed a hot-water spa on the deck behind the hotel and built a swimming pool next door.

MAGNOLIA HOTEL, 6529 Yount Street, Yountville, California 94599. Telephone: (707) 944-2056. Accommodations: double beds; private baths, some tub/shower, some shower only; no telephones; no television. Rates: $40 double, breakfast included. Meal Service: dinner Thursday through Sunday nights; wine only. No children. No pets. Cards: BA, MC. Open all year.

BURGUNDY HOUSE
Yountville

Charles Rouvegneau built Burgundy House in the 1870s to resemble the inns of the Saône, constructing 22-inch thick walls of fieldstone quarried from the Napa Valley hillsides. It was operated originally as a boarding house upstairs and a dirt-floored winery below. Over the years, the massive stone walls and hand-hewn posts and beams were plastered over or covered with dry wall; layers of linoleum covered the wood floors. Then in 1975, antique dealers Mary and Bob Keenan bought the old house for a shop. They restored the building to reveal the original stone and wood construction and used the upstairs rooms to display antique bedroom furniture. Much to the Keenans' surprise, customers started asking if they could stay overnight in these rooms, and before long the antique shop was converted to an inn.

Upstairs there are five bedrooms, each decorated distinctively with an eclectic assemblage of furnishings from many eras and many lands. To describe any room in detail would be an exercise in futility, for what you see today might not be there tomorrow. Every piece of furniture, every *objet d'art* in the inn is for sale. One honeymoon couple even purchased their bed! Two baths upstairs—also antique filled to include an old claw-footed tub—are shared by the guests. There is one bedroom downstairs, however, with a private bath and patio.

Also downstairs are common rooms for use by the guests. A large front room houses the Keenans' collection of unusual antique games. In back is a cheerful sitting room where a fire usually burns in the stone

40

Burgundy House

hearth and decanters of red wine and sherry are set out hospitably. At one end is a long pine table where guests are served a breakfast of fresh fruits, juice, coffee and luscious Venetian pastries.

The Keenans have also bought and restored a Victorian cottage down the road from Burgundy House. This accommodates four persons and is often booked in its entirety by a family or two couples traveling together. There is a bedroom with private bath and a bank of windows overlooking the vineyards. Another large room, also with bath, has a fireplace, its own sitting-room area and kitchenette. At this writing, plans are underway to construct another eight units next to the cottage.

BURGUNDY HOUSE, 6711 Washington Street, Yountville, California 94599. Telephone: (707) 944-2711. Accommodations: double beds; some private baths; no telephones; no television. Rates: $35-$40 single, $40-$45 double, continental breakfast included. No other meal service. Children in cottage only. No pets. Cards: BA, MC. Open all year.

WINE COUNTRY INN
St. Helena

Ned and Marge Smith had long dreamed of opening an inn in the wine country. For several years they spent vacations touring the inns of New England and getting ideas and advice. One warning they heeded: "Don't restore an old building, build a new one. There will be fewer headaches and more comforts." The Wine Country Inn, though constructed in 1975, looks like its been sitting on its hillock surrounded by vineyards forever. That's the way they wanted it to look. The two-story stone and wood structure with dormered windows and a gabled tower is a composite of ideas borrowed from historic buildings in the valley.

Comfort, however, is the key word here. All rooms are carpeted and have modern tile baths. The furnishings are antique, from a potpourri of periods, but the old four-poster beds have been widened to queen-size and the brass-framed doubles elongated. The rooms are papered with floral motif and each is different, but romantic in its own way. Eight of the rooms have freestanding fireplaces, four have patios, landscaped for privacy, and six have intimate balconies. Some have window seats in alcoves with views of the surrounding countryside.

Wine Country Inn

Downstairs is a large, homey common room, equipped with card tables and books on wine. Here in the mornings, at a long refectory table, a continental breakfast is served of fresh fruits and juices, assorted hot breads and coffee. On warmer days this repast is served on a deck outside.

WINE COUNTRY INN, 1152 Lodi Lane, St. Helena, California 94574. Telephone: (707) 963-7077. Accommodations: twin, double and queen-size beds; private baths, some tub/shower, some shower only; no telephones; no television. Rates: $35-$37 double, continental breakfast included; $6 for each additional person in room. No other meal service. No children under 12. No pets. Cards: BA, MC. Open all year.

Getting There: From Napa take Highway 29 two miles past St. Helena and turn right on Lodi Lane.

CALIFORNIA NEVADA

MINING COUNTRY

The Mother Lode
Across the High Sierra
To the Comstock Lode

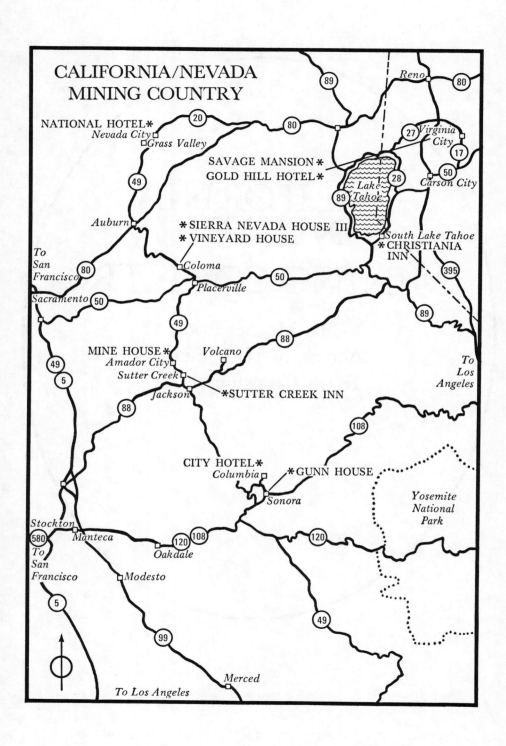

CALIFORNIA/NEVADA
MINING COUNTRY

NATIONAL HOTEL *
Nevada City
Grass Valley

89
Reno
80
80

SAVAGE MANSION *
GOLD HILL HOTEL *

27 Virginia
City
17
28
50
Carson City

Lake
Tahoe
89

Auburn

* SIERRA NEVADA HOUSE III
* VINEYARD HOUSE

South Lake Tahoe
* CHRISTIANIA
INN

To
San
Francisco
80
49

Coloma
50

Placerville
395

Sacramento
50

49

89

MINE HOUSE *
Amador City
Sutter Creek

Volcano
88

To
Los
Angeles

49

5

Jackson
* SUTTER CREEK INN

88

108

CITY HOTEL *
Columbia
* GUNN HOUSE

Sonora

Yosemite
National
Park

Stockton
580
Manteca
120 108
Oakdale
120

To
San
Francisco

5
Modesto

99

49

Merced

To Los Angeles

COLOMA

In the 1840s the only riches to be found in the Sierra Nevada came from the mountains' timber. But on January 24, 1848, the destiny of California was forever changed. On that day James W. Marshall was deepening the tailrace of a sawmill he had built with John W. Sutter at Coloma on the south fork of the American River in the Sierra foothills. While at work, he noticed in the raceway some glittering specks. These turned out to be gold and within months one of history's largest and most colorful gold rushes began. In the next decade some 100,000 prospectors would come to seek their fortunes in the Mother Lode.

A few years after Marshall's discovery, the town of Coloma had grown to over 10,000 inhabitants. But the prosperity of Coloma and of Marshall was short-lived. The gold of Coloma proved to be only a teaser for the vast wealth contained in the Sierra foothills to the north and south. Within a decade the ore here had been depleted and the miners went on to richer diggings. By 1868, only 200 residents remained and among them was a bitter and impoverished John Marshall, who survived by occasionally working as a gardener. Five years after his death in 1885, a large bronze monument was erected in his honor over the place of his burial.

What remains of the original town of Coloma is now preserved as the Marshall Gold Discovery State Park. There are mining exhibits, a replica of Sutter's sawmill and the cabin where Marshall lived.

Getting There: From San Francisco take Highway 80 to Sacramento, Highway 50 to Placerville, then Highway 49 north.

SIERRA NEVADA HOUSE III
Coloma

One of the 13 hotels which flourished in Coloma's prime was the Sierra Nevada House, unique among mining town hostelries for not having a saloon (a gold mine of its own in those hard-drinking days). Originally located next to the post office in old Coloma, the hotel was destroyed by fire in 1906, rebuilt the following year, and again perished in flames in 1926.

In 1963, a replica of the Sierra Nevada House was constructed on Highway 49, just north of the Gold Discovery State Park. There are six bedrooms with private entrances from the wide balcony which surrounds the building. They are rather sparsely furnished with 19th-century pieces, yet offer the creature comforts of today, such as modern baths and air-conditioning. The sagging mattresses, though, would seem to be from another century.

The dining room at the Sierra Nevada House is furnished in Victorian opulence, with fresh flowers on the table and snowy white cloths. The food, however, is no match for the setting. It's preferable to take your meals in the old-fashioned soda parlor in the front of the building, where the food is simple and the prices reasonable.

Despite some of its shortcomings, an overnight stay at Sierra Nevada House III is one of the best buys in the Mother Lode: A double room is only $15 per night and this includes a hearty breakfast of sourdough pancakes, orange juice and coffee.

SIERRA NEVADA HOUSE III, P.O. Box 268, Coloma, California 95613. Telephone: (916) 622-5856. Accommodations: twin, double and twin double beds; private baths with showers; no telephones; no television; electric heat; air-conditioning. Rates: $15 double, breakfast included. Meal Service: lunch and dinner in dining room; breakfast, lunch and dinner in soda parlor; full bar service April 1 to January 1. Children welcome. Pets allowed. No credit cards. Open all year except Mondays and Tuesdays from Labor Day until Easter.

VINEYARD HOUSE
Coloma

Robert Chalmers, owner of the original Sierra Nevada House in Coloma, built the Vineyard House in 1878 as a lavish residence for himself and his bride, a young widow, on vineyards she had inherited from her late husband, Martin Allhoff. Chalmers improved the original winery, built in 1866, and developed the vineyards to 500 producing acres. He was known for his extravagance. The house had 19 rooms with nine fireplaces and he spent the then exorbitant sum of $15,000 on furnishings. When the Marshall Monument was dedicated in 1890, Chalmers added a wing to the Vineyard House to provide space for a 10-course dinner for 2,000 people.

In his later life Chalmers allegedly became insane and locked himself in the basement where he starved to death. (There is some evidence, however, that he actually died elsewhere.) After Chalmers' death, his ghost was rumored to haunt the house, which fell into disrepair. The vineyards withered away and the old winery crumbled into ruins.

The Vineyard House was being operated as a run-down hotel and restaurant when it was discovered by Gary Herrera, an Oakland restaurateur who wanted to escape the metropolitan rat race. In 1975, Gary bought the property in partnership with his brother and sister-in-law, Darlene and Frank Herrera, and a friend, David Van Buskirk.

Thus began a gigantic, do-it-yourself restoration project. The four of them stripped floors and balustrades to the natural wood, papered walls, and hauled long-since forgotten pieces of period furniture down from the attic and refurbished them.

The dining room is filled with relics of yesteryear. A fire burns in a Franklin stove. Genuine kerosene-burning lamps flicker on tables topped with brown-and-white-checkered cloths. The dishes and flatware are a mishmash of patterns such as one might have inherited from a myriad of aunts. (Actually some of the chinaware came with the house, but much of it has come from doting customers who turn up with "grandma's dishes.")

The food is old-fashioned country cookery. Not always perfect, but always hearty and homemade. Pots of soup and big bowls of salad are set on the table and you serve yourself. The bread is freshly baked. Entrees include rib-sticking fare such as an enameled saucepan of

Vineyard House

simmering chicken topped with a two-inch layer of dumplings and gravy. Vineyard House does not serve a complete breakfast, but coffee and homemade bread are available for overnight guests.

Upstairs seven bedrooms are being renovated, though at this writing all were not completed. Each room is different, some with brass bedsteads, others with massive Victorian headboards. Homemade quilts top the beds. All the rooms will eventually be carpeted. None have private baths, but the community bath is above average for this type of inn: The walls are charmingly papered, the floor is simulated brick and there is a tile shower and built-in vanity.

The Vineyard House is very much a family operation, complete with a real grandma. Darlene Herrera's mother lives in the house and helps make the desserts. Her younger brother tends the bar. Her two sons are the "bellboys" and help bake the bread. And, as Darlene expresses it, "Everybody who comes here becomes automatic family."

VINEYARD HOUSE, P.O. Box 176, Coloma, California 95613. Telephone: (916) 622-2217. Accommodations: twin and double beds; community bath with tile shower; no telephones; no television. Rates: $12 single, $19 double, continental breakfast included. Meal Service: lunch and dinner during the summer, dinner only the rest of the year; wine only. Children welcome. No pets. Cards: AE, BA, MC. Open all year except Mondays and Tuesdays from September to June.

THE NATIONAL HOTEL
Nevada City

This veritable museum of Victoriana, now a National Historical Monument, is California's oldest continuously operated hotel. It was constructed in 1854, partially destroyed by fire, and completed in 1856, during the heyday of the gold rush. At that time Nevada City was the third largest town in California, with a population of 12,000, and the miners supposedly dropped $1,000 a day in the saloon of The National Hotel. It is said that the infamous dancer Lola Montez (the Countess of Lansfeld) and her young protégée Lotta Crabtree contributed to the revelry here.

Today, with a population of 2,000, Nevada City is a much quieter place, except for a freeway which unfortunately cuts through its hilly streets. Picturesque gas lamps enhance the forty-niner character of its main street.

In 1972, Dick and Florence Ness, self-confessed "antique nuts," bought The National Hotel and began the monumental project of bringing back its former splendor. Asphalt tiles were ripped off the floors and paint was stripped off the wainscotings to reveal the original natural woods in the bar and dining room. The lobby was refurbished with red-flocked wallpaper, Oriental rugs, crystal chandeliers and a square grand piano that was brought around the Horn. Rooms were brightened with floral wallpapers. And the old Victorian furniture was refinished—marble-topped tables, velvet-covered settees, canopied four-poster beds.

The hotel has 29 guest rooms, most of them occupying the second and third stories of the main brick building. The front rooms tend to be noisy, although several of these have private sitting rooms with French doors opening onto the wide balcony overlooking the street. In the rear, some of the rooms open into a bricked patio and garden. A few other rooms are located in a gazebo-like outbuilding behind the hotel—and overlooking the freeway. All have television; most have private baths and telephones. There is a small swimming pool.

In the hotel dining room, the gold rush era is rekindled by flickering coal lamps on the tables, Victorian furnishings, massive chandeliers. The dining room, however, is open only for lunch and dinner with a rather pedestrian menu: roast beef, steaks, lobster tail, fried chicken. But don't be disheartened; there's interesting dining nearby. At the American Victorian Museum, housed in a former foundry, you'll find weekend breakfasts hearty enough for the hungriest forty-niner; lunch and dinner are served, too. Also in Nevada City is Jack's Deer Creek Plaza where a variety of unusual dishes are offered in turn-of-the-century surroundings.

The National Hotel is a comfortable base for exploring the northern sector of the Mother Lode. In Nevada City itself, the American Victorian Museum is more than a restaurant; it houses a collection of historical books, documents, photographs and old mining equipment. More history exhibits are located in the gingerbread-trimmed Firehouse No. 1, and at Ott's Assay Office, where the miners reportedly brought a booty of $27 million in ore over the years.

Five miles from Nevada City is Grass Valley, where California's richest mines once produced over $400 million in gold. A mining

The National Hotel

display with a 31-foot waterwheel may still be viewed, as well as the homes of Lotta Crabtree and Lola Montez. Four miles from Grass Valley is the semi-abandoned town of Rough and Ready, which once tried to secede from the Union in protest of mining taxes. There is swimming and fishing in nearby lakes.

THE NATIONAL HOTEL, Nevada City, California 95959. Telephone: (916) 265-4551. Accommodations: twin, double, queen-size and king-size beds; 20 rooms with private baths, some tub/showers, 7 rooms with connecting baths; telephones in some rooms; television in all rooms. Rates: $14 single, $18-$20 double, $22-$30 suites; no meals included. Meal Service: lunch and dinner; full bar service. Children welcome. No pets. Cards: BA, MC. Open all year.

Getting There: Take Highway 80 through Sacramento to Auburn and Highway 49 north through Grass Valley to Nevada City.

AMADOR COUNTY

Located in the heart of the Mother Lode, this is one of California's smallest counties in both size and population, yet its mines yielded more than half the gold which came out of the entire Sierra foothills. Gold may still be panned in the streams and many of the old mines are open to the public. But today the commercial interests of the Amador-eans have turned from the mines to the vines. Amador County's Shenandoah Valley produces some of the state's most distinctive Zinfandel. And many of the wineries are open for touring and winetasting.

In Amador County, Highway 49 winds through oak-studded hillsides and the old mining towns of Amador City, Sutter Creek and Jackson. The brick or clapboard buildings, with their second-story balconies covering raised sidewalks, now house antique shops, art and craft galleries, saloons. A worthwhile side trip from Sutter Creek or Jackson is a visit to the picturesque mining town of Volcano, situated in a valley surrounded by pine-forested mountains above Highway 49.

The county contains two gold rush era hotels which have been in continuous operation since 1862: the St. George Hotel in Volcano, and the National Hotel in Jackson. Both have saloons, dining rooms and guest rooms furnished with antiques. Just south of the county line in Mokelumne Hill is another restored hostelry of the gold rush era, the

Leger Hotel. But the most outstanding accommodations in the area are found at Sutter Creek Inn and The Mine House, which are described in detail on the following pages.

It would be difficult to become bored in Amador County. Besides shopping, sightseeing, mine and wine touring, visiting historic museums, one may participate in a host of recreational activities. There is fishing and boating at nearby lakes Amador, Pardee and Camanche, and rafting on the Mokelumne River. There is hunting, tennis, a nine-hole golf course, and even skiing in nearby Kirkwood Meadows. And on summer evenings the Claypipers Theater presents old-time melodrama.

One also can eat well in Amador County. Jackson offers a number of family-style Italian restaurants, such as Buscaglia's, where the food is both hearty and above average. Jackson is also noted for the Argonaut Inn, located in the headquarters of the old Argonaut Mines. Here Katharine Sinclair cooks some of the most creative meals to be found in the entire Mother Lode. In Sutter Creek, The Brinn House, a charmingly restored Victorian next door to the Sutter Creek Inn, serves simple yet delicious lunches. And in Volcano, an exquisite breakfast or lunch will be found at the Jug and Rose, an ice cream parlor resurrected from the forty-niner era.

Getting There: From San Francisco take Highway 580 east through Tracy to Manteca, Highway 5 north to Stockton and Highway 88 northeast to Jackson. Sutter Creek is four miles north of Jackson on Highway 49; Amador City is two miles north of Jackson. This part of the Mother Lode may also be reached by taking Highway 50 to Placerville and proceeding south on Highway 49.

THE MINE HOUSE
Amador City

Over $23 million in gold bullion was removed from the Keystone Consolidated Mines in Amador City before they were finally closed in 1942. The mining company's offices, grinding and assay rooms were located in a two-story brick building on a hillside across the highway from the mines. In 1954 the building, then abandoned and run-down, was purchased by Marguerite and Peter Daubenspeck, who came to California on a vacation, were charmed by Amador and decided to stay. Originally the Daubenspecks intended to restore the old mine house for a residence; then they decided it would be an ideal inn.

After two years of renovation, the eight rooms were ready for guests. The Daubenspecks furnished the entire building with authentic period furniture, found within 100 miles of Amador City. And the rooms are handsome, indeed. There are burled-walnut pieces, Empire dressers, commodes topped with Italian marble, rockers, platform rockers, armoires, carved bedsteads and under each bed an old-fashioned bed warmer. Many of the rooms contain old pitchers and wash basins set on a commode. But this is for show only. The Daubenspecks have added modern wood-paneled baths throughout.

The rooms of The Mine House are named after their original usage. Downstairs is the Mill Grinding Room, where the ore was brought to be ground; the supports that held the shafts for the grinding machinery are still on the ceiling. Next door is the Assay Room, where the ore was evaluated for its gold content. There is a Retort Room, where the ore was stored, and a Stores Room that once contained the mining supplies. All the interiors are of painted brick.

The upstairs rooms, however, are the most attractive, with 13-foot-high ceilings paneled in redwood. On one side rooms open to a wide balcony overlooking the highway. On the other side they open to a covered patio dug out of the grassy hillside. These rooms originally housed the Keystone Consolidated Mining Company's offices and are appropriately named: Directors' Room, Bookkeeping Room, Keystone Room and Vault Room, which contains the safe in which the bullion was stored until the stagecoach transported it to San Francisco.

There is a swimming pool for guests at The Mine House. No meals are served, but each morning Peter Daubenspeck III (son of the original

56

owner) and his wife, who now own and manage the inn, leave a tray of orange juice and coffee by each door.

THE MINE HOUSE, P.O. Box 226, Amador City, California 95601. Telephone: (209) 267-5900. Accommodations: double and twin double beds; private baths with showers; no telephones; no television. Rates: $15-$24 single, $20-$24 double, $2 extra for each additional person in room, $2 for rollaway bed. Meal Service: orange juice and coffee included in room rate; no dining or bar facilities. Children welcome. No pets. No credit cards. Open all year.

SUTTER CREEK INN
Sutter Creek

"When I first saw this house, I fell in love. It was just like falling in love with a person," confesses Jane Way, vivacious proprietor of the Sutter Creek Inn. This instant love occurred back in 1966, while Jane was motoring through the Mother Lode with her children. The house was not occupied, but she sleuthed its history. When built in 1859 by a man named Keyes for his bride, this was the biggest house in town. Later it was the home of State Senator Voorhies, and in 1966 the house was still owned by his descendents—who refused to sell. For two months Jane Way persisted with phone calls. Finally, when she was about ready to give up, she was informed that the family had agreed to sell. And the Keyes-Voorhies House was rechristened Sutter Creek Inn.

Jane Way, a woman of enormous talent and energy, has changed far more than the name. She has dressed up every inch of the inn with a riot of color and charm. The gracious living room, painted a pale aqua, is comfortably furnished with large sofas upholstered in floral print, a hutch filled with antique china, a small piano and a grandfather clock. A chess set and a decanter of sherry by the fireplace are ready for the guests' enjoyment.

But the highlight of a stay at Sutter Creek Inn is breakfast in the country-kitchen/dining room. Walls, partially brick, partially paneled, are hung with copper colanders, an Oriental rug, a collection of guns. Two long, polished plank tables are gaily set with orange mats, gold-rimmed china and a pewter pitcher filled with dried flora. Shuttered windows look out to the lawn and gardens. Jane carries on an animated conversation with guests as she cooks, serves and pours a shot of brandy

Sutter Creek Inn

into the coffee. Her menu is ambitious: fresh fruit, perhaps berries, or peaches just picked from the inn's own trees. Jane might whip up pancakes with chopped nuts and apples, corn bread or a soufflé. And if it falls, who cares?

In the inn's early days, the only rooms rented were the small upstairs bedrooms, which are the least desirable today. The demand is for the outbuildings in the rear of the house—the woodshed, carriage house, storage shed and old laundry house, which Jane has extensively remodeled and furnished with flair.

Four of these have "swinging beds," actually suspended by cables from the ceiling. This was an idea she picked up in the tropics of Mexico where people often hang their beds to avoid crawling insects and lizards. But if you suffer from motion sickness, you won't need Dramamine; the beds may be stabilized easily.

No two of the rooms are alike, except that they are perfectly appointed down to the tiniest details: books, magazines, a deck of cards, a decanter of sherry. In one you might find a fireplace, in another a Franklin stove, in yet another a sunken bathtub. Some open out to private patios or porches, others into the lovely back garden. Some are furnished in solid Early American maple, others have canopied four-poster beds, still others contain brightly painted wickerware. Jane transforms whatever she finds around the countryside: an old drum topped with a wicker tray for a table, a miner's scale for a planter, a milk can for a lamp base, two water barrels for the base of a bathroom sink. All is visual joy.

Though there is much to see and do in the Sutter Creek area, Jane admits that most of her guests come primarily to relax, to get away from it all. "When there is bad news in the world, my business increases."

SUTTER CREEK INN, 75 Main Street, Sutter Creek, California 95685. Telephone: (209) 267-5606. Accommodations: twin, double and queen-size beds; all private baths; no telephones; no television. Rates: $26-$32 double, weekdays; $32-38 double, weekends; $55 for two-bathroom carriage house; breakfast included. Meal Service: breakfast for guests only; no lunch or dinner served. Children discouraged; children under 10 not allowed. No pets. No credit cards. Reservations accepted only for minimum of two nights on weekends; deposit of $20 per night required. Open all year except first two weeks of January.

COLUMBIA AREA

Columbia was one of the most prosperous gold rush towns, with ore taken from its fabulously rich mines valued at over $80 million. Within three years after gold had been discovered in 1850 at Hildreth's Diggings, as it was then called, the town's population had grown to some 20,000 and ranked as the second largest city in California. In its heyday Columbia boasted 40 saloons, 150 gambling houses, eight hotels, four banks and two volunteer fire companies! Despite their efforts, most of the original frame structures were destroyed in two early fires and the town was almost completely rebuilt in brick.

The Columbians' paranoia about fire has benefited posterity. The durability of these brick buildings caused the State of California to purchase the town in 1945 and restore it as the Columbia Historic State Park. Today, except for an onslaught of tourists, the tree-shaded Main Street with its boardwalks and balconied buildings looks much the way it did in the 1860s. No automobiles are allowed in the town itself, but a stagecoach does lumber through offering visitors a ride. The old blacksmith shop, harness and saddle shop, carpenter shop and a Chinese herb store are in working condition. And the historic Fallon House Theater comes back to life for six weeks each summer as a repertory playhouse for University of the Pacific students.

But the most unusual journey into yesteryear is found not in Columbia but at nearby Jamestown. This is the departure point for the Sierra Railroad's excursions aboard an old-time, steam-powered passenger train. During the day the train takes passengers on short jaunts through the foothills above Jamestown and Sonora. But a truly memorable train trip is found on the Sierra Supper Special, a leisurely five-hour excursion through the foothills west of Jamestown with cocktails, dinner and live entertainment on board. The food doesn't quite match the nostalgia, but it doesn't seem to matter to the railroad buffs on board. The Sierra Supper Specials run only on Saturdays in May, June and September through November, with shorter evening runs in the midsummer months. Reservations are strongly advised: Contact Great Western Tours, Sheraton-Palace Hotel, San Francisco, CA 94105.

Another way to tour this area of the Mother Lode, as well as the high Sierra, is by air. From Columbia airport Tuolumne Air conducts 75-minute flying tours over the central Mother Lode and Yosemite National Park. Yosemite Airlines operates day-long or overnight tours

City Hotel

to Yosemite via Pine Mountain Lake. For more information: Tuolumne Air or Yosemite Airlines, Columbia, California 95310.

Other recreational activities in the area include tennis, fishing, hunting, swimming and waterskiing in nearby lakes, horseback riding, golf, and river trips down the Stanislaus. But the true attraction of Columbia remains its gold mine of Early California history.

Getting There: From San Francisco, Highway 580 past Tracy to Manteca; Highway 120 east past Knights Ferry to intersection of Highway 108; Highway 108 east to Sonora; Highway 49 north to Columbia. By plane there are flights on Monday, Wednesday and Friday from San Francisco and Oakland via Yosemite Airlines to Columbia Airport, where there is a shuttle bus to the town of Columbia.

CITY HOTEL
Columbia

One of the old brick buildings restored by the state in Columbia is the City Hotel, with its wrought-iron balcony overhanging the sidewalk of Main Street. Built in 1856 by George Morgan, the hotel was called the "What Cheer House" until it was ravaged by fire in 1867. Four years later it was rebuilt as the Morgan Hotel and three years later the name was changed to City Hotel.

In the 1940s the State of California acquired the City Hotel as part of Columbia Historic State Park, and after spending $800,000 on restorations and furnishings, opened its nine bedrooms, dining room and saloon to paying guests. The operation of the hotel is unique in California. The young chambermaids in their "granny caps," the waitresses in their long last-century dresses, the waiters and busboys in their black ties are not the college students off on a lark usually found at resort hotels. They are all serious students of the Hospitality Management Program at Columbia Junior College, which operates the hotel as an on-the-job training facility.

The bedrooms have been impeccably furnished with massive burled-wood Victorian bedsteads framing comfortable brand-new mattresses, brass coat racks, marble-topped bureaus. The rooms have half baths, no shower or tub, but the hotel thoughtfully provides each guest with a "bathroom caddy," a basket containing soap, washcloth, shower cap and even terry-cloth shower shoes. The trip down the hall to the shower is made as pleasant as possible here.

Upstairs there is also a homey old-fashioned parlor decorated with flocked paper, Oriental rugs and Victorian settees. There is a small library and games for the guests' use. A continental breakfast is served here each morning.

Downstairs is the What Cheer Saloon and a gracious high-ceilinged dining room, a serene setting for the magnificently appointed tables set with cut-glass goblets, graceful wineglasses of varying sizes, flowered service plates, small brass hurricane lamps and even silver napkin rings on the sparkling white napery.

The food here is far removed from the mountain-country cooking you might expect to find in the Mother Lode. The City Hotel's kitchen is run by a first-rate chef from San Francisco and his menu would come as no surprise in New York or Paris. But in Columbia? There are escargots and fresh bluepoint oysters baked with a sauce mornay among the appetizers. Kentucky limestone lettuce and hearts of palm compose some of the salads. Shrimp bisque, French onion gratinée and vichyssoise comprise the choice of soups. Then there is a choice of 16 elegant entrées: chicken poached in wine with oranges and mushrooms, veal with apples and cream sauce, chateaubriand with a sauce béarnaise, and a loin of lamb stuffed with spinach are but a few. Dinners are à la carte and you will probably spend at least $12 for a memorable meal.

CITY HOTEL, P.O. Box 1870, Columbia, California 95310. Telephone: (209) 532-1479. Accommodations: twin, double and twin double beds; private half baths, community showers; no telephones; no television. Rates: $27.50-$39.50 double, continental breakfast included. Meal Service: continental breakfast served in parlor, no lunch, dinners; full bar service. Children discouraged. No pets. One night's deposit required with reservation. Cards: BA, MC. Conference facilities for 25 available. Open all year; dining room closed on Mondays.

The Gunn House

THE GUNN HOUSE
Sonora

Sonora is only four miles south of picturesque Columbia, but a century away in atmosphere. Although some of the old adobe and frame buildings still stand as a testament to Sonora's original Mexican settlers and gold rush past, the town today is a bustling community living in the present. Nevertheless, a bit of the colorful history can be recaptured at the Gunn House.

The house is named for Dr. Lewis C. Gunn, who was lured from Philadelphia via Mexico to the California gold mines. Settling in Sonora he became the first county recorder and in 1850 started the Mother Lode's first newspaper, the Sonora *Herald*. Using Mexican laborers he built Sonora's first two-story adobe as home and office. During his 10 years of residence in Sonora, Gunn was a controversial figure. Once, protesting his editorial views, angry townspeople burned his printing press in front of his home.

Since Gunn's departure the house has been considerably expanded beyond its adobe core. For a while it served as a hospital. Later it was rechristened the Hotel Rosa Italia, a boarding house and restaurant where family-style dinners attracted a clientele from miles around.

In the early 1960s, Margaret Dienelt bought the house and began an ambitious restoration, adding a wing on the back containing more bedrooms and a living room. For nearly two years she searched the area for antiques: "I had to visit people's attics. There were very few antique shops in those days, but as word spread, people started calling me."

Today the 27 bedrooms are appointed with handsome antiques, quilted bedspreads, shuttered windows, private baths, televisions and telephones. Most rooms open out to the wide balconies which surround the building; the most desirable rooms, however, are those in the rear which open to a balcony or stone terrace and oval-shaped swimming pool. The spacious living room contains a large stone fireplace and a settee and davenport, which were shipped around the Horn by Margaret Dienelt's own grandparents.

Except for a morning repast of coffee and rolls, the Gunn House serves no meals.

THE GUNN HOUSE, 286 South Washington, Sonora, California 95370. Telephone: (209) 532-3421. Accommodations: twin, double, twin double and queen-size beds; private baths with tub/shower; telephones; television; air-conditioning; electric heat. Rates: $17-$31 double, continental breakfast included; $5 for each additional person in room. No other meal or bar service. Children welcome. Small dogs allowed; $5 refundable damage deposit for dogs. Cards: AE, BA, CB, DC, MC. Open all year.

CHRISTIANIA INN
South Lake Tahoe

Between the Comstock and the Mother lodes the Sierra Nevadas soar to pine-forested heights, which surround one of the largest and loveliest bodies of water in the West—Lake Tahoe. Nestled in the mountains high above the lake is a romantic and luxurious European chalet—the Christiania Inn. Located at the base of the Heavenly Valley ski lift, the Christiania was built in 1965 as a rustic ski lodge emulating a Norwegian pension. Until recently the accommodations were somewhat rudimentary, despite the old world charm. Then in late 1976, a major facelifting inside and out was started to transform the Christiania into the epitome of luxury. At this writing not all of the rooms have been completed but the work should be finished by the fall of 1977.

All of the eight rooms will be suites, some two-storied, with deep carpeting and views of the mountains or pine forests through leaded-glass windows. Each living room will have a wood-burning fireplace, a wet bar concealed in an armoire and a library stocked with books. Bedrooms are being opulently appointed with canopied beds, covered with hand-woven spreads, set on raised platforms. Baths will have separate vanities, tiled tubs and showers, even a private steam room. Telephones, color televisions, coffee pots, a decanter of sherry—every amenity will be there.

In the lower floor of the Christiania there is a large and comfortable lounge with views of the mountains above. In the mornings a fire blazes cheerily in the large stone fireplace and guests start the day with freshly squeezed orange juice, croissants and coffee. In late afternoons, during ski season, the bar attracts a convivial after-ski crowd, but at other times of the year it is a quiet retreat for cocktails.

The dining room also offers views of the mountains, a cheerful fire and some of the best food to be found at South Lake Tahoe. Dinners include soup, freshly baked bread, a choice of some 10 entrées, which range from beef Wellington to country-style ribs, followed in the European tradition by salad and a selection of fresh fruit and aged cheeses. The wine list is extraordinary, with some 3,000 bottles which include European imports and the aristocrats of California's small premium wineries. The Christiania's new wine cellar is often the site of private tastings and special dinners for parties of 24.

Christiania Inn is a short drive from a myriad of recreational activities at Tahoe's South Shore. The ski lifts of Heavenly Valley are only 100 yards away. In summer there is swimming and water skiing at the lake's many beaches, hiking, horseback riding, tennis at public courts. And year-round there are the attractions—or distractions—of the State Line gambling casinos with their elaborate floor shows and big-name entertainers.

The South Shore is also teeming with restaurants. Among the best, besides the Christiania's own dining room, are Chez Villaret for French food in a provincial setting, and the Sage Room at Harvey's Resort Hotel at State Line for first-rate steaks. Guests at the Christiania, however, do not need advice on dining out. Patrick Robinson, the inn's affable and knowledgeable manager, is a reliable source on restaurants of the area. And there is even a concierge to make your reservations.

CHRISTIANIA INN, P.O. Box 6870, South Lake Tahoe, California 95729. Telephone: (916) 544-7337. Accommodations: two-room suites with living rooms and wet bars; all queen-size beds; private bathrooms with tub, shower and steam room; telephones; color television. Rates: suites from $75 double, older rooms not yet remodeled from $30 double, continental breakfast included. Meal Service: dinner daily, Sunday brunch; full bar service. No children. No pets. Cards: AE, BA, DC, MC. Open all year.

Getting There: From San Francisco take Highway 80 to Sacramento, Highway 50 through Placerville and South Lake Tahoe to Ski Run Boulevard (before State Line), turn up Ski Run Boulevard and follow the signs to Heavenly Valley, turning left near the top of the hill; Christiania Inn is across from the lifts at 3918 Saddle Road. From the southern Mother Lode, Lake Tahoe can be reached via Highway 88 from Jackson. By air there are daily flights to Lake Tahoe airport from San Francisco, Oakland and San Jose via Air California and from Los Angeles via PSA; the inn will send a car for guests arriving at the airport.

VIRGINIA CITY

Gold was found first here on the side of Mount Davidson, but the discovery of silver in 1859 was the big bonanza of the Comstock Lode, one of the richest ore deposits in the world. Over $300 million in precious metals was excavated within 20 years from the deep mines which still lie under the streets of Virginia City. This silver helped to finance the Civil War and to build the city of San Francisco. It also made millionaires of those who exploited the mines—James G. Fair, George Hearst, James Mackay, William Ralston and William Sharon to name a few.

In the 1860s and 1870s, Virginia City was queen of the West, second largest city this side of the Rockies, the richest boom town in America. Palatial mansions studded her barren hills. Extravagant entertaining was the order of the day (heaps of oyster shells and wine bottles still lie around the town). Fortunes in silver passed over the lusty bars of the Bucket of Blood and 109 other saloons. The most glamorous performers of the day played to bejeweled audiences at Piper's Opera House. And in 1862, a 27-year-old adventurer/prospector started writing of these lively events for the *Territorial Enterprise* under the pseudonym of Mark Twain.

In 1875, a fire destroyed much of Virginia City. Her mines by then were almost depleted. The boisterous miners who had courted her silver moved away. The stately buildings remaining disintegrated.

Today only about 700 people live in Virginia City and their bonanza is tourism. The main street is pure honky-tonk with one-arm bandits in the old saloons reclaiming the lost silver. But around the town many of the old mansions stand freshly painted, proud of their new prosperity, and open for visitors to relive the colorful past. Some of the abandoned mines may be toured. Piper's Opera House, Sutro's Tunnel and the offices of the *Territorial Enterprise* are among other sights to be seen. The Sharon House, in the heart of town, and Cabin in the Sky, between Virginia City and Gold Hill, are two of the better restaurants.

Getting There: From San Francisco take Highway 80 east to Reno, Highway 395 south to Highway 17 which leads south to Virginia City. From Lake Tahoe, take Highway 50 east through Carson City and Highway 17 north through Gold Hill to Virginia City.

The Savage Mansion

THE SAVAGE MANSION
Virginia City

Some $20 million in silver was unearthed from the Savage Mine, a pittance compared with Consolidated Virginia's big bonanza of $105 million. Yet the Savage Mine made a mark on history as the breakthrough point of the famous tunnel which Adolph Sutro built through Mount Davidson at a cost of $6,500,000 to drain and ventilate the Comstock mines. The Savage Mining Company also made its mark on the landscape of Virginia City by building one of the most splendid high-Victorian mansions to grace these hilly streets.

The three-storied gabled mansion was built in 1870 to house the mining company's offices on the first floor and the superintendent's family on the upper levels. The house was magnificently furnished, even by the Comstock's opulent standards, and was used to entertain notables of the era. General Ulysses S. Grant was a guest for two days in 1879; Thomas Edison is rumored to have been another visitor.

After the Comstock's silver was depleted, the Savage Mansion deteriorated along with the rest of Virginia City. By 1960 it was deserted and a veritable wreck, shingles missing from the mansard roof, paint almost totally peeled away, the foundation disintegrated. At this time it was purchased for a mere $7,500 by Elaine and Gerald Harwood, who had moved to Nevada from Redwood City. Restoration began and continued for nine years as the Harwoods duplicated the original detailing and reclaimed the mansion's furniture which had been sold to a nearby museum.

Today the Savage Mansion is owned by Ann Louise Mertz and Bob and Irene Kugler, who moved to Virginia City from Southern California seeking an active retirement project—"We didn't want to just play golf for the rest of our lives." They have continued the restoration to near-mint condition while living there, and conduct tours of the building. The third floor rooms can be rented by those who wish to savor the romance of the Comstock era. Among the three guest rooms is the one that was occupied by General Grant. The room is supposedly the way it was then, with floral wallpaper, a pot-bellied stove and an awesome bedstead that extends to ceiling height.

Guests share a bathroom which retains the plumbing of the 1880s—a toilet with overhead tank and a six-foot-long copper tub. The music room and formal parlors on the second floor are open to overnight guests. And in the morning, coffee and rolls are served in the Victorian kitchen.

SAVAGE MANSION, South D Street, Virginia City, Nevada 89440. Telephone: (702) 847-0574. Accommodations: double and twin double beds; community bath with tub/shower; no telephones; no television. Rates: $30 double, continental breakfast included. No other meal or bar service. Children discouraged. No pets. Cards: MC. Open all year.

GOLD HILL HOTEL
Gold Hill

Over the hill south of Virginia City are the remnants of the little town of Gold Hill, once an important mining center. Here is the oldest hotel in Nevada still existing, the Gold Hill Hotel, built in 1859. The tavern of the hotel was a popular gathering place during the Comstock boom. Mark Twain and his cronies used to drink here before their meetings at the Odd Fellows Hall next door. And a prominent judge of the era, dressed in white tie and tails, was accidentally shot at the bar after attending a performance at the Piper's Opera House; another guest was cleaning his loaded gun and it fired, hitting the judge.

In 1956 the Gold Hill Hotel was purchased by Fred Immoor and his wife Dorothy, an interior decorator. "We loved antiques, so we bought one big one!" At that time it bore little resemblance to the original building. The thick stone walls had been covered with layers of plaster and plaster board. The Immoors were determined to undo 100 years of "improvements" and make the hotel look as rustic as it did in the 1860s. "We've been working on it for 20 years, and we only have 100 years of work ahead of us."

Upstairs the five small guest rooms are partially papered and partially paneled with century-old wood, and furnished in the style of the mid-19th century. The Bridal Suite has a four-poster bed with a white canopy; other rooms contain bedsteads of solid brass. There are marble-topped commodes with bowls and pitchers, gilded rococo mirrors. The community bath has a vintage claw-footed tub.

Downstairs the Immoors have exposed the original stone walls, wooden ceiling and brick floors of the tavern. There is a brick and stone fireplace, a stone bar and everywhere you look a plethora of antiques—

cast-iron stove, spinning wheel, coffee grinder, a player piano circa 1880, kerosene-burning lamps.

The Immoors provide dinner for groups of 10 or more in the tavern at three long narrow tables covered with oil cloth. It's a simple, do-it-yourself affair. Guests barbecue filet mignons over coals in an old blacksmith's forge, then help themselves to bread and potatoes baked in a wood-burning stove. There is salad and cheesecake, too.

Because there must be a group of at least 10 for dinner and because the hotel accommodates just 10 overnight guests, Dorothy Immoor says Gold Hill is at its best when five couples get together and take it over for a weekend. There's not much privacy here and "that way it's just like a friendly house party."

GOLD HILL HOTEL, P.O. Box 304, Virginia City, Nevada 89440. Telephone: (702) 847-0111. Accommodations: double beds; community bath; no telephones; no television. Rates: $15 double, morning coffee included. Meal Service: dinner for groups of 10 or more; full bar service. Children welcome. No pets. No credit cards. Open all year.

CALIFORNIA NORTH COAST COUNTRY

San Francisco
To the Redwood Empire

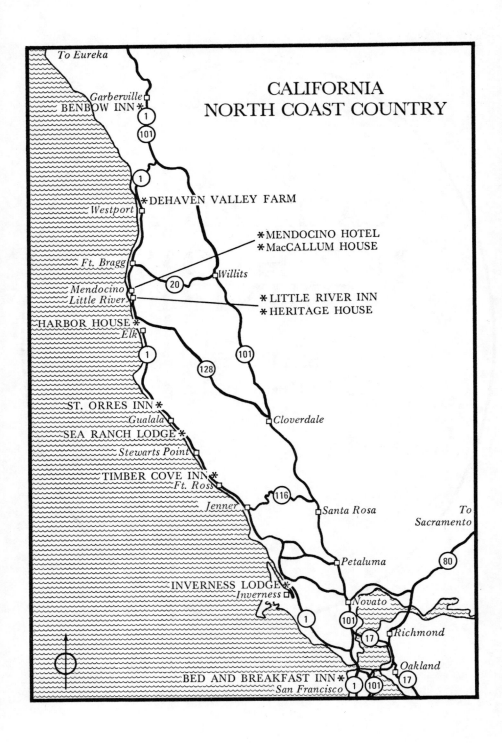

CALIFORNIA
NORTH COAST COUNTRY

To Eureka

Garberville
BENBOW INN ✱
① ⑩①

①

✱ DEHAVEN VALLEY FARM
Westport

✱ MENDOCINO HOTEL
✱ MacCALLUM HOUSE

Ft. Bragg   Willits
⑳
Mendocino
Little River   ✱ LITTLE RIVER INN
                      ✱ HERITAGE HOUSE
HARBOR HOUSE ✱
Elk
①
⑫⑧   ⑩①

ST. ORRES INN ✱
Gualala   Cloverdale
SEA RANCH LODGE ✱
Stewarts Point

TIMBER COVE INN ✱
Ft. Ross
⑪⑥
Jenner   Santa Rosa   To
                                        Sacramento

                      Petaluma   ⑧⓪

INVERNESS LODGE ✱
Inverness   Novato
                      ⑩①
                      ⑰   Richmond

                                  Oakland
BED AND BREAKFAST INN ✱   ⑰
San Francisco   ① ⑩①

BED AND BREAKFAST INN
San Francisco

San Francisco is the eye through which the threads of California history have converged. Spanish missionaries first brought Western culture here in 1776. But it was the fortunes in gold from the Mother Lode in the 1850s and later the silver from the Comstock that built the magnificent city by the Golden Gate. To her teeming port came the European immigrants who planted California's fertile valleys with grapes and returned their wines to San Francisco's splendid tables. And from the redwood forests to the north came the lumber for the gingerbread houses that cover her hills and valleys.

It is thus fitting that in one of these brightly painted Victorians, in the heart of a city renowned for its hospitality, is one of the most charming and romantic country inns in the West.

Robert and Marily Kavanaugh knew for many years that, when their children were raised, they would start an inn patterned after England's "bed and breakfast" guest houses. And they were determined the locale would be on one of San Francisco's quaint cul-de-sacs. "They are so like the English mews," says Marily. Finally they found the perfect house, a pre-earthquake Victorian a few doors up Charlton Court from the fashionable shops and restaurants of Union Street. Marily has discovered the house had been a boarding house at times in its history. In fact she thinks it might even have been built as a guest house, and quoting Hesse comments, "I like to think that 'everything changes and everything returns.' We have recycled the house back to its original purpose of serving people."

Robert Kavanaugh is a realtor and a builder; Marily has an extra-ordinary flair for decorating. Combining their talents, they remodeled, painted and decorated with family heirlooms from England, combined with vividly colored contemporary accents. The Kavanaughs moved into the top floor and opened the two lower stories to guests in 1976.

Marily welcomes her guests with the warmth of an old friend and soon they feel like one of the family. (Those who were strangers on arrival write thank you notes after a stay with the Kavanaughs signed "fondly" or "with love.") Upon your arrival you are offered sherry from a crystal decanter on a silver tray in the sitting/breakfast room. A Windsor table is set with Copeland china which belonged to Marily's grandmother. English country prints are on the wall. There's a white wicker settee with deep cushions covered in a floral print. Flowers and plants everywhere. A spinning wheel in the corner.

Each of the five bedrooms has a distinctive name and color theme inspired by the boldly patterned quilts which cover the beds. Green Park is splashed in colors of lime, green and blue. Next door, Kensington Gardens is done in restful tones of coral and sand. Both open to a redwood balcony and deck behind the inn. There are three more rooms in a brick-walled lower level brightened with white paint and gay colors. The Willows resembles a forest in springtime, with a leafy-print fabric covering the bed and curtaining two studio beds hidden in alcoves. Autumn Sun looks like a shogun's bedroom, with quilts patterned in ochre stripes and blazing red mandalas; a window looks into a Japanese garden. And the bedroom named The Library houses a fine leather-bound collection of the works of Charles Dickens.

In all of the rooms, Marily's gracious touches are found. A bouquet of fresh spring flowers on the nightstand. A bowl of fruit and selection of current magazines on a table. Beds turned down to reveal the pretty printed sheets and pillowcases. And on each pillow—a fortune cookie.

Breakfast is as important as the beds here. Marily serves juice, freshly ground coffee, hot croissants or occasionally "sticky buns," on her antique flowered chinaware. Some guests prefer to be served in the breakfast room or outdoors on umbrella-covered tables in the flower-

The Bed and Breakfast Inn

Inverness Lodge

filled garden. But Marily prefers to pamper you with a breakfast tray in bed. "I had no training in running an inn, but it's really no different than having guests in your home."

THE BED AND BREAKFAST INN, 4 Charlton Court (off Union between Buchanan and Laguna), San Francisco, California 94123. Telephone: (415) 921-9784. Accommodations: twin, double, queen- and king-size beds; three community half baths with tub/shower and stall shower; no telephones; no television. Rates: $25-$35 double, continental breakfast included; add $5 for summer and holiday rates, June 1 to September 30; five percent discount for one week stay. No other meals or bar service. Children discouraged. Pets discouraged. No credit cards. Open all year.

INVERNESS LODGE
Inverness

Manka and Milan Prokupek came to California from Czechoslovakia by way of Holland and British Columbia, where they had a restaurant. In 1956 they opened Manka's Restaurant in Inverness Lodge, a rustic inn on a wooded hillside above Tomales Bay. Manka's rich Czech-Viennese dinners soon brought people from all over the San Francisco Bay Area to the village of Inverness. Many were delighted to discover that they could rent rooms here rather than drive back late to their homes.

The brown-shingled lodge, built at the turn of the century, contains four small, pine-paneled rooms upstairs. They are comfortably appointed with maple furniture, quilted bedspreads, wing chairs and flowered curtains. Two of the rooms open to large, private sunny decks with chaises and boxes of primroses. There are four other rooms in a rustic red cottage behind the lodge; these share a patio edged with ivy, azaleas, camellias; from the back windows look out to a forest of oaks and giant rhododendrons. Then there is a private cottage, set off by itself in a garden of calla lilies and nasturtiums. Inside there is a bright red Swedish stove set on a brick hearth and two studio couches in a homey living area. A double bed is partitioned off in a sleeping area. And there is an equipped kitchen, too. Perfect for families.

Inverness Lodge is now managed by Milan Prokupek, Jr. and his wife, Judy, who does the cooking, though Manka herself still makes the luscious pastries. The dinners start with a visit to a lavish buffet of hors d'oeuvre—Norwegian and Dutch herring, Danish cheeses, sausages, cold meats, fresh fruit, relishes and several salads. Then comes a cream soup and a choice from among eight Czech or Viennese entrées, ranging from roast duckling with caraway sauce and veal with paprika sauce to fresh oysters from Tomales Bay baked with anchovy butter. Complete breakfasts are served, too, with tempting choices like French toast with cinnamon pears, or crêpes filled with raspberry preserves. The dining room is rather plain, but large windows offer views of the woods. It is the verdant setting that imparts a special magic to Inverness Lodge, rather than the rooms themselves.

The lodge is but a few miles from Point Reyes National Seashore, 53,000 acres of coastal wilderness with magnificent hiking trails and beautiful beaches. Here a model village has been built, typical of those inhabited by the Miwok Indians who once dwelled on these shores. And here also is the harbor which sheltered Sir Francis Drake's Golden Hinde for six weeks during his expedition to the Pacific in 1579.

The small resort town of Inverness has many picturesque shops and arts/crafts galleries. Boats may be rented for sailing or fishing in Tomales Bay. And just down the road from Inverness Lodge is Vlasta's, another fine Czech restaurant.

INVERNESS LODGE, Callender Way and Argyle, Inverness, California 94937. Telephone: (415) 669-1034. Accommodations: double beds, some rooms with studio couch as well; private baths with tub only; one cottage with kitchen and bath with stall shower; no telephones; no television. Rates: $16.50 double, $20.50 for cottage; no meals included. Meal Service: breakfast and dinner, wine and beer only. Children welcome. No pets. Cards: AE, MC. Open all year except Tuesday and Wednesday; also closed Monday and Thursday in the winter.

Getting There: From San Francisco take Highway 101 north to San Anselmo turnoff; continue on Sir Francis Drake Boulevard (Highway 17) through Fairfax, Olema and Point Reyes Station to Inverness. Inverness Lodge is just beyond the town, on the left. For a longer, but more scenic drive, take Highway 101 to Mill Valley, then Highway 1 through Stinson Beach and Bolinas to Point Reyes Station.

TIMBER COVE INN
Jenner

North of Jenner, where the Russian River meets the Pacific, Highway 1 plunges upwards, switchbacking through mountainous terrain, then stretches north high on the hills above the ocean. Here is Fort Ross, the site of a Russian seal-and-otter-trapping settlement for three decades in the early 1800s. Three miles north of Fort Ross, perched on the cliffs above the Pacific, is Timber Cove Inn. During the 1880s, this cove was an important shipping point for timber from the forested mountains above. Today only an old cemetery remains. And only the pounding of the surf on the rugged coast punctuates the serenity.

Timber Cove Inn was designed and built in 1963 by Richard Clements, a UC philosophy graduate, who describes himself as a "self-taught architect." The inn was intended as a social center for the surrounding 800 acres that he was developing into vacation home sites. In the dramatic lobby, massive poles soar upwards some 40 feet to a cathedralesque beam ceiling. A gigantic stone fireplace dominates one end of the room; floor-to-ceiling glass, the other. From a balcony above, doors open into some of the sleeping rooms. Windows on one side permit a glimpse of a tranquil Japanese garden and reflection pool. Miniature pines. Pieces of sculpture. A little bridge. On the other side, beyond a long bar, is the dining room. Stone walls. Ocean view. Pretty tables, set for just two.

Timber Cove Inn was conceived as a romantic retreat for lovers. Many of the 46 rooms have sunken Roman tubs within the bedroom itself. These are the most popular rooms, too. "If I had it to do again, I'd have a sunken tub in every room," Clements admits. Almost all of the rooms (and some of the tubs) command views of mountains, craggy shore line and sea. All are rustic design with exposed poles and beams, walls of natural wood or whitewashed barn siding. Bright Danish rugs give a splash of color to cement floors. There are Swedish fireplaces in some of the rooms.

Only two meals a day are served at Timber Cove Inn. There is a substantial brunch with choices ranging from cheese blintzes with strawberry preserves to abalone steak with eggs. At night the menu assumes continental overtones with a dozen or so entrées ranging from cannelloni and rack of lamb to filet of sole marguerite.

Timber Cove Inn

Recreational activities in and around Timber Cove are limited, though golf, tennis and riding are within reach. Fort Ross, which has been recently rebuilt as it was in Russian days, lures history buffs to its museum and nature lovers to its rhododendron park. Nightlife, other than a convivial drink in the inn's own lounge, is nonexistent. But the isolation of Timber Cove is the main attraction. As Clements expresses it, "The essence of Timber Cove Inn is that it is a place of peace and beauty, a place to forget worry, a place to get to know yourself again, or someone else, a place to think or meditate . . . and not least, it is a place to be in love."

TIMBER COVE INN, North Coast Highway, Jenner, California 95450. Telephone: (707) 847-3231. Accommodations: double, twin double, queen-size and king-size beds, waterbeds; private baths with tub/shower; no telephones; no television. Rates: $33-$60; no meals included. Meal Service: brunch and dinner; full bar service. Children welcome. Pets allowed. No credit cards. Open all year.

Getting There: Take Highway 101 north to Petaluma; take Washington Street exit to road leading to Bodega Bay; then proceed north on Highway 1 past Jenner.

THE SEA RANCH LODGE
The Sea Ranch

Up the coast from Timber Cove is The Sea Ranch, which was once part of a 17,000-acre Mexican land grant, Rancho de Herman. In the 1960s, Castle & Cooke began developing 5,000 acres of this land as home sites and constructed The Sea Ranch Lodge on a high meadow which juts out into the Pacific. The contemporary buildings of resawn wood are now acquiring the silvery patina of age. The main building houses the dining room, with its two-story ceiling thrusting upward at interesting angles and its windows viewing the Pacific. Here is also a spacious lounge with comfortable custom-designed black naugahyde couches and chairs, cube tables painted in primary colors, a stone fireplace, views of the sea.

The lodge bedrooms cluster around a fenced-in, landscaped compound. And they are probably the most luxurious modern accommodations along California's rugged north coast. The upstairs rooms are preferable, with better views and dramatically high, sloping ceilings. All rooms have twin double-size beds, covered with handsome woven fabrics, wall-to-wall carpeting, contemporary furniture of natural woods. Many have fireplaces, sitting-room areas, built-in window seats from which to gaze at the sea.

The Sea Ranch dining room serves three "no-nonsense meals" daily with no pretentions to "gourmet" cooking. There are sandwiches and salads for lunch; seafood, steaks and chicken for dinner.

Guests at the lodge have full privileges to use the facilities of Sea Ranch. There are seven private beaches, miles of trails through meadows and forests, excellent rock fishing and surf fishing. There is also a pool, sauna, tennis and golf. Some rooms have enclosed pet yards.

THE SEA RANCH LODGE, P.O. Box 44, The Sea Ranch, California 95497. Telephone: (707) 785-2371. Accommodations: twin double-size beds; private baths with tub and shower; no telephones; no television. Rates: $23-$33 single, $27-$38 double ($3 less off season), $4 each extra person in room; no meals included. Meal Service: breakfast, lunch and dinner; full bar service. Children welcome. Pets allowed. Cards: BA, MC. Open all year except Christmas.

ST. ORRES INN
Gualala

Midway up the coast between Jenner and Mendocino is an astounding piece of architectural sculpture: a miniature Russian palace rendered in hand-carved redwood, with onion-top turrets and stained-glass windows. A relic from the Russian settlers of over a century ago? No. St. Orres Inn is the creation of two young men from Marin County who painstakingly handcrafted every detail.

Eric Black and Richard Wasserman met at school in Mill Valley and worked together on several carpentry projects. Then they acquired a decrepit garage overlooking the Pacific on property once owned by the St. Orres family who homesteaded this area. For four years they scavenged wood from beaches and old barns, collected pieces of stained glass, sawed, hammered and sculptured their inn, which finally opened in early 1977.

Through a patio and trellis-covered terrace you enter a cozy parlor with oval windows, tapestries on the walls, furnishings of the last century. It would be no surprise to see Anna Karenina pouring tea by

St. Orres Inn

the stone hearth. An oak door leads to a spectacular dining room over which the domed turret rises some 50 feet. From high above, light filters down from stained-glass clerestories while three tiers of multi-paned windows provide glimpses of forest and sea through a cascade of hanging plants. Chocolate-brown carpeting, rust-colored tablecloths and primitive stoneware made by local potters complete the setting.

Black describes the inn's menu as czarist court food, which of course translates as French *haute cuisine*. There is filet mignon, encased with pâté and puff pastry, bathed with sauce madeira; veal medallions with a creamy mustard sauce; filet of sole stuffed with shrimp and served with a sauce nantua. Desserts are sinfully rich—try the chocolate decadence. There is a fine wine cellar, too, with carefully selected California premium varietals sharing space with French Grand Cru bottlings. In the mornings a complimentary breakfast of fruit, scones and pastries is served to the overnight guests.

Upstairs the wood-paneled bedrooms are simply appointed with furnishings designed and built by Black and Wasserman. The beds are covered with patchwork or appliqued quilts made by a local crafts-person. The front rooms have private balconies and ocean views. Guests share a commodious bath.

St. Orres Inn has its own private beach across the road. In season you can pick abalone from the rocks or fish for steelhead. On weekends there are flea markets and local arts/crafts festivals to be explored. But, as in most inns along the north coast of California, the reason for coming here is the isolation, peace and beauty.

ST. ORRES INN, P.O. Box 523, Gualala, California 95445. Telephone: (707) 884-3303. Accommodations: double beds; community bath with shower; no telephones; no television. Rates: $25-$45, continental breakfast included. Meal Service: lunch and dinner; wine only. Children welcome. No pets. Cards: BA, MC. Open all year.

Getting There: Follow directions to Timber Cove Inn and proceed north on Highway 1 past Gualala.

HARBOR HOUSE
Elk

This stately house was built on the cliffs above Greenwood Landing by the Goodyear Redwood Lumber Company in 1916 as an executive residence and for entertaining business guests. In those days the small port below was heavily trafficked by schooners coming for their rich cargoes of lumber from the nearby Albion forests. In fact the house itself is an enlarged replica of a redwood model house, designed by Louis Christian Mullgardt for the 1915 Pan American Exposition in San Francisco.

When the lumber boom came to an end in the 1930s, Harbor House was converted to an inn, which had become run-down in recent years. In 1975 Rick Sutfin, a school superintendent, and his wife Pat, a teacher, acquired the house and moved to Elk from the San Francisco Peninsula, seeking an alternate to suburbia. "We want to make our guests feel as though they are visiting a friend's country home. Our goal is to recreate the Edwardian atmosphere which once permeated each redwood board." And so they have done.

The walls, vaulted ceiling and fireplace of the gracious living room are entirely paneled with hand-carved and hand-fitted redwood, still preserved by its original finish of polished hot beeswax. Furnishings are comfortable and eclectic—overstuffed chairs, a large Persian rug, a Steinway piano, Chinese chests and tables, bookcases bulging with reading matter.

There are five spacious bedrooms in the house itself, four with fireplaces, and another four cottages built on the edge of the bluff next to the main building. With paint and flowered wallpapers, antiques, four-poster beds, the Sutfins have restored these rooms to their original charm. Some of the cottage rooms have French cast-iron fireplaces, set on brick hearths; some have private terraces overlooking the ocean.

Among the traditional characteristics of country inns are home-cooked meals, leisurely served, the Sutfins believe. They share the cooking, making all the soups, breads, salad dressings and desserts from scratch. "Sara Lee does not live down the street!" Breakfast and dinner are served in a spacious dining room with a panoramic view of the Pacific and the large tunneled rocks in the harbor below. The morning meal includes juice, fruit and perhaps shirred eggs, omelets or eggs benedict. At evening, the entrées are often fresh seafood—broiled salmon or deviled red snapper. A selection of wine and beer is available.

Harbor House is only 20 minutes by car from Mendocino's shops and art galleries. But most guests choose to spend their time exploring the inn's private beach, following a little stream to a 25-foot waterfall cascading into a secluded grotto. In the evenings the Sutfins encourage conversation and song around the fireplace.

HARBOR HOUSE, P.O. Box 167, Elk, California 95432. Telephone: (707) 877-3203. Accommodations: twin, double and king-size beds; private baths with shower or tub/shower; no telephones; no television. Rates: $53-$65, full breakfast and dinner included. Wine and beer available. No children. No pets. No credit cards. Open all year.

Getting There: Follow directions to Mendocino, but turn south on Highway 1 and drive south through Albion to Elk.

HERITAGE HOUSE
Little River

In this ivy-covered inn with its many cottages rambling over hillsides, meadows and gardens down to the sea, L. D. Dennen and his wife Hazel strive to preserve the heritage of the Mendocino coast. Dennen's own roots are implanted in the history of the area. His grandfather, John Dennen, who had come from New England, built the inn's main building as a home for rancher Wilder Pullen in 1876. In the 1890s Pullen advertised that the 160-acre sheep and cattle ranch and the seven-room house was for sale; for the land, buildings and livestock he was asking $7,000. In the early 1930s neighbors started to eye the former Pullen house with suspicion: Baby Face Nelson was using the cove below the house for his bootleg operations and, before his arrest, had concluded one of his last deals inside the house. As recently as the early 1940s, Chinese immigrants were smuggled into the country here.

In 1949, L. D. Dennen bought the house his grandfather had built and turned it into an inn. Over the years, the Dennens have added cottages on the meadows below the original house, building some anew, moving others from elsewhere in the countryside. All have names like Schoolhouse, which the Dennens built with lumber salvaged from the Greenwood School in Elk; the school's sign serves as a headboard and

BUILT 1877 AD

Heritage House

the children's desks as bedside tables. Firehouse, Barbershop, Ice Cream are some other names. Recently the Dennens have converted an old water tower, brought down from Mendocino, into a two-story unit with a circular stairway leading from a living room to a balconied bedroom. There are 50 units altogether now, some with brick fireplaces or Franklin or pot-bellied stoves. All have private baths.

Some years back Dennen acquired an old apple storage house from a nearby farm for $75 and rebuilt it next to the 1876 house as a bar. There is a magnificent ocean view from here and from the adjoining lounge with its walk-in fireplace. The dining room also has large windows overlooking the cottages and gardens below. The ambience is more conservative than at other inns in the area; guests are requested, though not required, to wear jackets at dinner.

The Dennens make no epicurean claims about their kitchen and aspire only to good American food—and lots of it. The menu changes each night, but a typical dinner would be: beef and barley soup, fresh pear and cheddar salad, a choice of chicken with sesame seeds or ginger-glazed corned beef, accompanied with buttered potatoes and peas and freshly baked orange biscuits; for dessert, chocolate mousse. Breakfasts are hearty, too: There's a buffet of fruits, juices and cereals, followed by a country breakfast of eggs, grilled sausage and pan gravy, fresh biscuits and fried potatoes. Heritage House operates on semi-American plan only; breakfast and dinner are included in the rates.

HERITAGE HOUSE, 5200 Highway 1, Little River, California, 95456. Telephone: (707) 937-5885. Accommodations: twin, double and king-size beds; private baths, some tub/shower, some stall shower; no telephones; no television. Rates: $50-$90 double, breakfast and dinner included. No lunch is served; full bar service March through November; wine and beer only during February. Children welcome. No pets. No credit cards. Open February through November.

LITTLE RIVER INN
Little River

In 1853 pioneer lumber and shipping tycoon Silas Coombs built an impressive New England-style mansion for his family on a hillside above Little River Cove, bringing much of the furnishings around the Horn from his native Maine. In 1929, as the lumber business diminished, the Coombs family turned the house into an inn, which has been expanded to 50 rooms and is run by Silas' great-grandson today.

The mansion, faithfully maintained in its original style, houses an antique-filled parlor and, upstairs under dormered roofs, four floral-papered and shuttered bedrooms. There is also a rustic no-frills Western bar with leather-covered booths and a large, modernized dining room. The old house is now the nucleus for a complex of garden cottages, a motel-style annex, and a golf course where Silas' orchard once stood.

Many of the garden cottages are two-bedroom units, wood paneled and furnished in Early American style. Some have fireplaces and private decks. A few have kitchenettes. All have views of the gardens or the sea.

The annex rooms all have sliding glass doors leading to a balcony with a beautiful view of the sea. All have twin double-size beds (some queen-size) and the newer rooms have a tub as well as shower.

In the early days of the inn, the Coombs family served their guests abalone picked from the rocks in the cove below. Now, of course, the abalone comes from Mexico but Little River Inn still is noted up and down the coast for its rendition of this delicate shellfish. Ling cod and sole from local waters, pan-fried oysters, salmon in season and steaks comprise the balance of the dinner menu, served with soup, salad, homemade rolls and cobbler. A salad-and-sandwiches lunch is also served and a hearty breakfast.

LITTLE RIVER INN, Little River, California 95456. Telephone: (707) 937-5942. Accommodations: double, twin double, queen-size and king-size beds; private baths, some with tubs as well as showers; no telephones; no television; some kitchenettes. Double rates: $24 rooms in inn, $24-$38 cottages, $32 new annex, $40-$60 suites, $5 per extra person in room, $5 crib; no meals included. Meal Service: breakfast, lunch and dinner; full bar service. Children welcome. No pets. Reservations on weekends accepted for two nights only. No credit cards. Open all year.

Little River Inn

MENDOCINO

Cabrillo discovered Cape Mendocino in 1542 and named it after Don Antonio de Mendoza, first viceroy of New Spain. But except for its name, nothing about the coastal village of Mendocino is Spanish. Situated on a rocky bluff which projects into the Pacific, the town looks like a movie set of a New England village, reflecting the heritage of its founders. Except for fresh paint, time has not touched the Victorian clapboards, set among windmills, water towers and windswept cypress trees. Behind rise the redwood-forested mountains of the Coast Range.

It was this precious timber which attracted the early settlers to the Mendocino coast. Harry Meiggs, a San Francisco lumberman, brought the first sawmill to Mendocino from the East aboard the brig Ontario and the lumber boom began. Others harvested the seafood from these northern waters, and started a fishing industry which still flourishes in the nearby harbor of Noyo. In the late 19th century, some 3,500 people lived in Mendocino, which then boasted eight hotels, 17 saloons and as many bordellos.

Today the population is only 1,100, among which are many artists and craftspeople. The entire town has been declared an historic monument so that its character will be preserved. Along Main Street, which faces the sea, and along picturesque side streets, where hollyhocks climb over picket fences, there are 17 art galleries and crafts shops. Within the area are tennis courts and a nine-hole golf course. The surrounding waters offer deep-sea and stream fishing, and canoeing.

Just north of Mendocino is Fort Bragg, a lumber town built on the site of a military post which was established in 1857. Fort Bragg is the departure point for the Skunk railroad, a scenic six-hour journey inland along the Noyo River, through 40 miles of redwoods. Advance reservations may be made by writing California Western Railroad, Box 907B, Fort Bragg, California 95437.

There are a number of good restaurants in the Mendocino area. Two of the most outstanding are in the village of Little River south of Mendocino. The Ledford House, located in an old farmhouse overlooking the ocean, serves dinners inspired by Mediterranean cuisine; the Little River Cafe is a tiny French bistro set behind the post office. Reservations at both should be made days in advance.

Getting There: From San Francisco take Highway 101 north through Santa Rosa to Cloverdale; Highway 128 north to the coast where it joins Highway 1. Elk is a few miles south on Highway 1; Little River, Mendocino, Fort Bragg and Westport are located north on Highway 1. Driving time to Mendocino is about three and one-half hours.

MENDOCINO HOTEL
Mendocino

In 1878, one of the houses on Mendocino's Main Street was bought by San Franciscan Ben Bever; his family and furnishings later arrived by schooner. That fall the *Mendocino Beacon* broke the news that Ben Bever was building an addition to his house and starting a boarding house. "It shall be called the Temperance House and no liquor shall be served." Bever's brother Sam joined him in the enterprise, and the name was changed to Central House, later Central Hotel and finally Mendocino Hotel.

During the last five decades the hotel has changed hands frequently. Even though it was shabby, the hotel was still regarded fondly by locals as a meeting place. In 1973, San Diego businessman R. O. Peterson, founder of the Jack in the Box chain, bought the hotel and renovated it to a level of luxury that had not existed before. Even in its prime years, the hotel had been nothing fancy, just a comfortable hostelry for loggers and traveling salesmen. Peterson retained architect Wayne Williams and his wife Paula, an interior decorator, to invest the hotel with the elegance of the Victorian era. Polished dark woods and wainscotings, flocked wallpapers, Oriental rugs and Tiffany-style glass were installed in the lobby and dining room. A spectacular dome of genuine Tiffany, found in Philadelphia, is suspended over the carved wooden bar. (Temperance most certainly is not the house rule today.)

Upstairs 24 bedrooms have been renovated to mint condition and decorated with bright flowered wallpapers, canopied or brass beds, marble-topped dressers, Victorian chairs. Many rooms have views and balconies. A few have private baths, but lack of one is not so critical here. The community baths are modern and immaculate and the hotel even provides terry-cloth robes for your trip down the hall.

Hotel guests receive a complimentary breakfast of freshly squeezed orange juice, home-baked nut-and-fruit breads, and coffee. For lunch and dinner the hotel dining room is open to the public, serving acceptable but not inspired fare, with emphasis on fresh sea-foods from neighboring Noyo. An attractive, plant-filled greenhouse room has been added off the main dining room.

MENDOCINO HOTEL, P.O. Box 587, Mendocino, California 95460. Telephone: (707) 937-0511. Accommodations: twin, double and queen-size beds; some private baths, community baths with showers; no telephones; no television. Rates: $40-$55 double with bath, $25-$35 double without bath, continental breakfast included. Meal Service: lunch and dinner; full bar service. Children welcome. No pets. Cards: BA, MC. Open all year.

MacCALLUM HOUSE
Mendocino

Lumber magnate William H. Kelley owned much of the town of Mendocino in the 1880s. So when his daughter Daisy married Alexander MacCallum in 1882, Kelley built the young couple a honeymoon house even finer than his own home. The three-story Victorian with gingerbread gables had a wide porch where the MacCallums could sit and watch the lumbermen float their logs down Big River into the Pacific. Daisy matured to become the matriarch of Mendocino and much of the town's social life revolved around her home.

In 1974 San Francisco stockbroker William Norris and his wife Sue bought the house from the MacCallum family and transformed it into an inn. All of the handsome original furnishings were still intact—Tiffany lamps, Persian rugs, carved footstools, paintings and an enormous library of turn-of-the-century books. Everywhere you look—in the dining room, in the halls—there are old leather-bound books ranging from William James' *Varieties of Religious Experience* to romantic novels to works in Latin and German. "There must be three or four thousand books," Sue Norris guesses. "I've never counted them all."

The Norrises papered the upstairs bedrooms with flowered prints reminiscent of the Victorian era, hung matching curtains and installed new mattresses, covered with handmade quilts, on the old carved-oak beds. In the third-floor attic there is a little sitting room where white-curtained windows provide a view of the town.

Downstairs a bar opens to an enclosed section of the porch where multipaned windows look to the sea. In the dining rooms there are large

95

MacCallum House

cobblestone fireplaces; oil lamps and fresh flowers are on the tables. During the first year of operation the Norrises ran the kitchen themselves, but subsequently they have leased it to Tim Canon and Al Feifer, who have provided an extensive menu with entrée choices ranging from rack of lamb and Cornish game hen to freshly caught salmon. A continental breakfast of orange juice, warm nut bread and coffee is served to the inn's guests.

Many of the shrubs planted by Daisy—gigantic flaming geraniums, pink and purple roses, rhododendrons—still thrive in the MacCallum gardens. Recently the Norrises have converted some of the garden structures into living quarters for their guests. The old greenhouse is now a rustic cottage, with a Franklin stove installed. The water tower has become a two-story guest house with a pot-bellied stove and ocean view. The carriage house contains two separate units with fireplaces. And surrounded by a sea of flowers is a gazebo, once the playhouse of the MacCallum children and still furnished with child-size chairs. Yes, you can stay here, too.

MacCALLUM HOUSE, P.O. Box 206, Mendocino, California 95460. Telephone: (707) 937-0289. Accommodations: twin and double beds; community baths, some tubs, some tub/shower, some stall shower; no telephones; no television. Rates: $24.50-$34.50 double, continental breakfast included. Meal Service: dinner and full bar service from April through December; breakfast all year. Children welcome. No pets. Cards: AE, BA, MC. Open all year.

DEHAVEN VALLEY FARM
Westport

"We only wanted to move to the country. We had no notion of opening an inn," say Rachel and Jim Sears, innkeepers of the Dehaven Valley Farm on the coast north of Mendocino. But when they discovered this Victorian farmhouse—then long-abandoned and condemned—they wanted to buy it. "It was too big for the two of us, but we thought it would make a perfect inn. Now the income enables us to stay here. We're not doing this to get rich." After some three years of hard work ("we papered, painted or carpeted every inch"), the young couple opened the inn in 1974.

Dehaven Valley Farm

The six bedrooms look like a *House Beautiful* version of a 19th-century farmhouse: old wooden dressers with porcelain wash basins and pitchers, white cafe curtains at the double-hung windows, towels hanging from an antique rack, a bowl of daisies and nasturtiums on the nightstand. Walls are covered with pretty floral papers and hung with old prints intermingled with brightly colored collages, the work of Rachel, a former art student. The front bedrooms, upstairs under a dormered roof, overlook a pasture where the Sears' sheep graze. Beyond is the sea. You can hear the surf at night and awake in the morning to the gentle baaing of the sheep.

You also awake to the smell of freshly ground and brewed Viennese coffee from Rachel's big sunny kitchen below. Breakfasts are leisurely events at Dehaven Valley Farm, with guests seated together around two large oak tables in the cheerful dining room. Rachel joins the conversation as she replenishes the coffee and baskets of just-baked bran rolls. You delight in little details—a sprig of nasturtium on your butter plate. Juice, coffee and rolls are complimentary. But for a nominal charge there is a country breakfast of waffles, bacon and eggs.

Dinners are served only on Friday and Saturday nights and they are a six-course feast. You start with an appetizer—perhaps spinach crêpes with a cheese sauce, stuffed grape leaves topped with yogurt, or a soufflé. After soup comes the main course—often seafood caught that morning at Noyo, served with vegetables just picked form the Sears' garden. Then there is salad, cheese and fruit, plus dessert.

The attraction of Dehaven Valley Farm for most people is not the activities offered, but the *lack* of them. If you become restless, Mendocino is about 40 minutes by car. But Dehaven visitors seem content to walk along the beach, to follow the old logging road to an abandoned lumber town, or to browse in the Sears' well-stocked library.

DEHAVEN VALLEY FARM, P.O. Box 128, Westport, California 95488. Telephone: (707) 964-2931. Accommodations: twin and double beds; community baths, tub and shower; no telephones; no television. Rates: $20 double, continental breakfast included. Meal Service: full breakfast daily; dinner on Friday and Saturday; wine only. No children under 12. No pets. No credit cards. Open all year.

Getting There: Follow directions to Mendocino and continue north on Highway 1 through Fort Bragg and two miles past Westport.

BENBOW INN
Garberville

South of Garberville, Highway 101 follows the south fork of the Eel River as it flows through valleys edged with unusual red rock formations and groves of giant redwood trees. This is logging country, fishing country, rustic camping country. Then the valley widens and at its head the Eel River snakes into a lake. There—lo and behold—stands a four-story English Tudor manor house.

The Benbow Inn, with its formal half-timbered construction and gabled roof seemed even more incongruous in these forested mountains when the Benbow family built it in 1926. The Benbows, five sisters and four brothers with no prior hotel experience, dammed the river to create a lake and commissioned San Francisco architect Albert Farr to design the inn on its shores.

Today it's a step back to the 1920s as you enter the stately lobby with its high timbered ceiling, carved woodwork, Oriental rugs, massive sculptured stone fireplace and sturdy antique furniture. One would almost expect Scott Fitzgerald to step through the French doors onto the formal oak-shaded terrace to admire the statuary or observe a game of croquet in progress on the lawn beyond. Fitzgerald might not have slept here, but in the inn's heyday the Benbows did host the likes of John Barrymore, Charles Laughton, President Herbert Hoover and Mrs. Eleanor Roosevelt.

The Benbows sold the inn in 1952 and after a decade of decline it was purchased by retired advertising executive Albert Stadler, who restored the inn to its former grandeur, adding many antiques from his private collection. In 1974, Stadler sold Benbow to Dennis Levett and Cornelius Corbett who have continued the improvements.

Off the lobby is a comfortable bar where you can get as high on nostalgia as on the spirits. Photographs of vintage 1920 airplanes and classic cars adorn the paneled walls. And from a jukebox in the corner come the sounds of Glenn Miller, Freddy Martin, Artie Shaw, Wayne King and others from the era of big bands.

Beyond the bar is a sun room where a buffet lunch is served. Guests eat breakfast and dinner on the terrace or in the large half-timbered dining room where multipaned windows look out to the gardens and river. The dinner menu is continental/American with a

Benbow Inn

selection of some dozen entrées ranging from beef Stroganoff to southern-style baked ham.

The inn's 40 bedrooms offer a choice of sleeping arrangements. The second- and third-story rooms are probably the nicest, all with views of the surrounding terrain from large windows or bays. Most are appointed with painted and gilded French furniture. A few contain some valuable and handsome pieces of Hepplewhite with intricate wood inlays. But the fourth floor rooms, originally reserved for servants, have a distinctive "garret" charm of their own. They are quite cozy with dormer windows; a few have sitting rooms, although most do not have private baths. Most popular with families, however, are the two floors of rooms under the terrace. Though not as light and sunny as the upper rooms, they are interconnecting and open directly outside so the children can easily come and go.

Despite its remote location, Benbow offers a variety of recreational facilities. There is a nine-hole, par-36 golf course, fishing, hunting and hiking trails. In years when the Rain God permits the lake to be filled, there is swimming from the inn's private beach, canoeing and paddle boating. Seven miles south of Benbow is Richardson Grove State Park, one of California's most important redwood preserves.

BENBOW INN, Garberville, California 95440. Telephone: (707) 923-2124. Accommodations: twin, double, queen-size and king-size beds; most rooms have private baths, tub/shower or shower only; some share connecting baths or community baths down the hall; no telephones; no television except in lobby. Rates: $16-$24 double; no meals included. Meal Service: breakfast, lunch and dinner; full bar service. Children welcome. Dogs allowed. Credit cards: AE, BA, MC. Open April 1 to December 1.

Getting There: Benbow Inn is 200 miles north of San Francisco, two miles south of Garberville, on Highway 101. From the Mendocino coast, Benbow may be reached by Highway 1 to Ligget and then north on 101. The inn will send a car to Garberville airport for guests arriving by private plane.

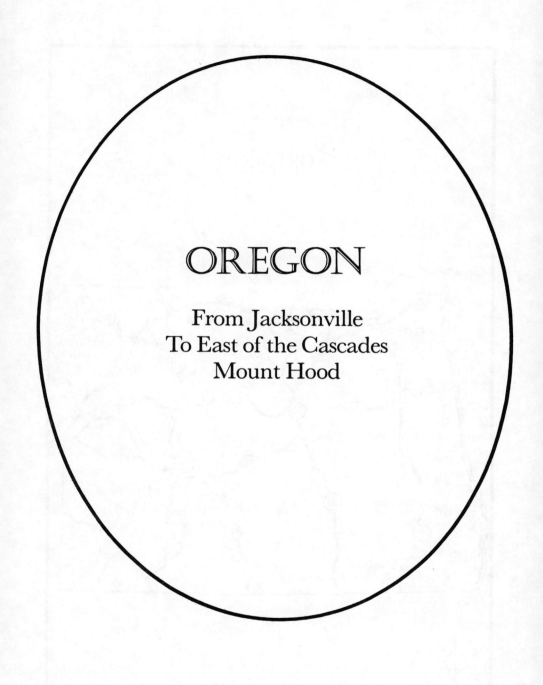

OREGON

From Jacksonville
To East of the Cascades
Mount Hood

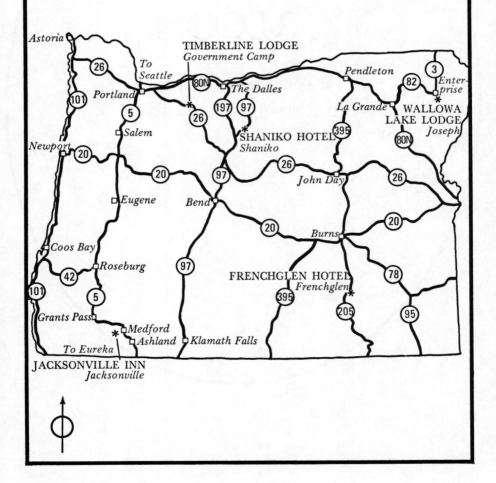

OREGON

JACKSONVILLE INN
Jacksonville

If you've been hankering to visit an Oregon gold rush town that began its life over 100 years ago, yet remains very much alive today, you would do very well in Jacksonville, Oregon, at the Jacksonville Inn.

Jacksonville began with the gold rush of 1851 and many of its original 1850s-vintage buildings still stand as first constructed. Even today, new buildings must be constructed in frontier style.

The Jacksonville Inn, one of the veterans, is a two-story brick building erected in 1863 as a mercantile store by Messrs. Ryan and Morgan. Later it housed a bank, hardware store, professional offices and a furniture repair shop. It once had four floors, the upper two of wood, but these were lost somewhere along the way. The bricks were made in the local Jacksonville kiln, one of the town's early industries.

The inn's restaurant (the Dinner House) has been drastically remodeled but even so there are hints of the past. Walls are still the original brick, with specks of gold visible in the mortar. Since logging played a dominant role in Jackson County's past, relics such as cross-cut saws and peaveys are featured in the decor. And as this is orchard country, the lounge ceiling is made of smudge pots. (This new cocktail lounge, with adjacent private banquet room and dance floor, can cater to parties of 100.)

The Dinner House menu offers prime rib, steak and seafood most of the time, and such specialties as beef burgundy and veal Français. There's also a good vegetarian plate.

The eight bedrooms are rather small but each has private bath and all are different, charmingly furnished with antiques acquired in the area: brass bedsteads, oak highboys with beveled mirrors, Boston rockers and a few oak bedsteads with five-foot-high headboards. All rooms are air-conditioned.

You can start sampling 19th-century frontier architecture next door to the inn. The United States Hotel (now housing a historically recreated and functioning bank) was built in 1880. Rutherford B. Hayes was at the opening festivities. Nearby (almost everything is nearby in Jacksonville) is the handsome Pioneer Courthouse where more than a few horse thieves and claim jumpers met speedy justice. It's now a fine museum and houses valuable archives and artifacts. The Beekman Bank closed its doors back in 1915, but is now maintained for visitors, with much original equipment on display.

A walking tour will give you a chance to observe these and dozens of other historic sites and structures (homes, stores, churches), listed and described in a little brochure prepared by the Ashland Historic Preservation Committee. Or ask at the inn, or ask almost any of the town's 2,000 residents what to see. Even a trip to the Jacksonville Cemetery can spark your imagination with vivid insights into the Old West. Consider these inscriptions on headstones: "Killed by a grizzly bear," or "Hanged for a killing."

The whole area abounds with events and attractions for the tourist. The annual Peter Britt Gardens Music and Arts Festival offers classical music for every taste for three weeks each August. Chamber music and recitals are held in the ballroom of the United States Hotel, orchestral concerts in the beautiful gardens which were planted by the Swiss immigrant Peter Britt in the 1850s. The audience sits on the grass and on folding chairs on a broad sloping lawn surrounded by stately trees and native and semitropical flower gardens.

Within driving range of Jacksonville are the Oregon Caves, a bit farther (77 miles) is lovely Crater Lake National Park, and 21 miles away is Ashland, site of the internationally known Shakespeare Festival. Theatrical productions are held in Ashland year-round. The two regular seasons are Stage 2, from February to April, and the famous summer series, predominantly Shakespeare, from June to September.

The nearby Rogue River country is spectacular, drawing hunters and fishermen from around the world, the former in search of ducks, pheasant and deer, the latter, of trout, bass and steelhead.

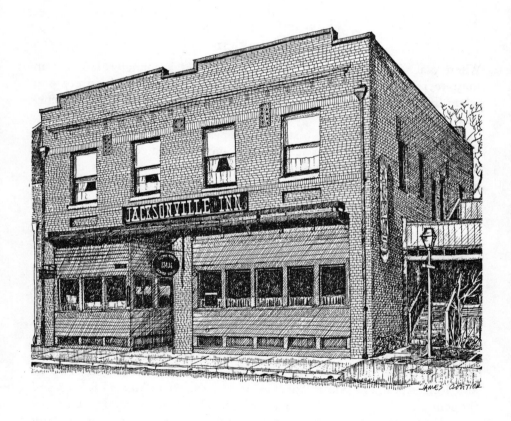

Jacksonville Inn

JACKSONVILLE INN, 175 East California Street, Jacksonville, Oregon 97530. Telephone: (503) 899-1900. Accommodations: twin, double and twin double beds; private baths with showers; no telephones, no television. Rates: $14-$16 double; no meals included. Meal Service: breakfast and dinner year-round, lunch in summer; full bar service. Children welcome. Pets discouraged. Cards: BA, MC. Open all year.

Getting There: From Portland, 290 miles south on Interstate 5 through Grants Pass to Medford, then seven miles west on 238. From Ashland, north on Interstate 5 to Medford and as above.

FRENCHGLEN HOTEL
Frenchglen

When you visit the historic, recently reopened Frenchglen Hotel, you may feel you've stepped back through time to a more leisurely era, when life was simpler and people entertained themselves without benefit of mass media.

Built in 1914, the two-story hotel was used to accommodate the overflow of visitors to the nearby "P" ranch. The screened veranda still seats visitors after the evening meal; the living room holds a piano, guitars and books and magazines. Meals are served family style and feature good country home cooking, including home-baked bread. There are no menus; cook's choice may be Southern baked ham, chicken and dumplings, prime rib or turkey. It's a good idea to make reservations for meals.

The Frenchglen Hotel is a place for the nature lover, not the person seeking luxury accommodations. In fact, not much has changed at the hotel since the early days, except for the addition of indoor plumbing. The eight bedrooms are small but very comfortable. The mattresses are good, and the beds have colorful handmade quilts.

Once belonging to the Bureau of Sports Fisheries and Wildlife Department, the hotel is now owned by the Oregon Division of Parks and Recreation as a State Wayside. It was leased to Malena Konek and reopened to the public in 1976 after being closed for several years.

The name "Frenchglen" is a combination of the names of Peter French and Dr. Hugh Glenn. Peter French arrived in the Blitzen Valley in 1872 with a herd of cattle and six Mexican vacqueros. He acquired the squatter's rights of a man named Porter, got financial backing from his father-in-law, Dr. Hugh Glenn, and built an empire of 132,000 acres around his home base at the "P" Ranch. French raised cattle and horses, fought Indians and droughts and storms. His life came to a dramatic end in 1897 when he was shot from his horse by a neighbor-competitor.

In 1935, the "P" Ranch land became a part of the Malheur National Wildlife Refuge. The ranch house is gone, except for its chimney, but the old barn still stands, with gnarled, solid juniper posts supporting it, and a weathered plank door on 90-year-old iron hinges.

A primary attraction to visitors here is the wildlife refuge. The refuge museum, 28 miles north of Frenchglen, has specimens of most of the 264 species of birds found in the area. This is one of the country's most important wildlife refuges, a much-frequented stop on the Pacific Flyway. Birdwatchers should try to be here during the peak of the spring waterfowl migration (mid-March to early April) or in October. They may expect to see ducks, cranes, Canada geese, snow geese, whistling swans, sandhill cranes, herons, avocets—and maybe a white pelican. The songbird migration is at its peak in mid-May.

The Blitzen Valley runs through the refuge. From near the hotel, you can start a 42-mile auto tour of this fascinating valley. A fine interpretive guide, put out by the Malheur Refuge, tells you what to look for and where: the spot where Pete French was murdered, a recent volcanic crater, nesting sandhill cranes. Throughout the area, deer, antelope, muskrat, beaver, mink, raccoons and coyotes abound and can often be seen.

Another attraction for visitors to Frenchglen is Steens Mountain, directly to the east. This geologically interesting mountain (a true fault block peak) is 30 miles long and rises over 9,600 feet, falling sharply to the Alvord Desert on its east side. The mountain was named for Major Enoch Steen, who was sent in 1860 to protect settlers from the Indians and determine the practicality of a road from southeast Oregon to the Willamette Valley. This was Paiute Indian country, and those with patience to explore may find stories carved in rock and possibly arrowheads. However, artifacts are protected by Federal law and may not be collected or disturbed. Take pictures instead.

Hiking and backpacking into the Steens Mountain Recreation Lands will take you from the dry, treeless sagebrush-sprinkled plain through the juniper-clad, rocky canyons, on to aspen groves and finally into the alpine high country with wildflowers and open meadows.

Frenchglen Hotel

Don't try to get to the top except between mid-July and October—there's likely to be too much snow other times.

Steens Mountain's lakes and rivers have been stocked with rainbow, brook and Lahontan cutthroat trout; anglers will also find plenty of the native redbow trout. As for hunting, there is an occasional season for big-horn sheep (recently re-established on the east side of Steens Mountain); pronghorn antelope and mule deer are also around, as well as game birds—sage grouse, mourning doves, quail and chukars.

Hunting and angling seasons and limits are under special regulation of the Oregon Fish and Wildlife Commission; check with the Portland office (1635 S.W. Alder Street) or local license agents.

FRENCHGLEN HOTEL STATE WAYSIDE, Frenchglen, Oregon 97736. Telephone: (503) 493-2565. Accommodations: twin, double and queen-size beds; community baths with showers; no telephones; no television. Rates: $13 double, $14 double with twin beds, $16 double with queen-size bed (subject to change); no meals included. Meal Service: breakfast, lunch and dinner; no bar service. Children welcome. No pets. No credit cards. Open all year with possible exception of January and February; call to check.

Getting There: By car, from Portland, 26 to John Day, 395 to Burns, from Burns take 205 south to Frenchglen (60 miles). From Bend, 20 then 395 to Burns; to Frenchglen as above. From Nevada, 95 then 78 to Burns, to Frenchglen as above. Nearest airport and bus station are at Burns.

WALLOWA LAKE LODGE
Joseph

This comfortable, three-story rustic lodge at the south end of Oregon's Wallowa Lake would be a restful spot to hole up in for a few days and restore the soul with lazy days on the lake and evening strolls beneath mighty evergreens. But the temptations of the area's varied outdoor activities are so strong that you might never find time for a do-nothing day. Best idea is to come for longer than a weekend, since you're traveling so far anyway.

The 50-year-old lodge is typical of the best old inns of the Northwest: unpretentious, roomy, informal, just enough modernization

111

over the years to keep guests happy, and no effort to emulate a Holiday Inn. For instance, with that lovely lake at your doorstep, who needs a swimming pool or a sauna? To be sure, certain local entrepreneurs have introduced such facilities in the neighborhood as a Go-Kart track, a roller-skating rink, miniature golf, and some alpine-type gift shops; but these are all easy to avoid.

The lodge has a very large lobby with fireplace to scale, card tables and a make-yourself-at-home atmosphere. The Nez Perce Room (cocktail lounge) is on a lower level. The spacious dining room serves hearty breakfasts and smorgasbord-style dinners—the latter from 1 pm to 8 pm on Sundays—but not lunch. Box lunches may be requested for outings.

The 20 rooms in the lodge are on the second and third floors. Most have connecting bath between two rooms. They are adequately furnished with little effort to follow any particular decorating scheme. No easy chairs or antiques, but the beds are good. Besides the lodge rooms there are several kinds of cabins, all with private bath. Some are simply sleeping rooms; some are log cabins with kitchenette, electric heat, fireplace and two or three bedrooms; and others, similar but larger and newer, are on the Wallowa River. These last will accommodate up to 10 persons.

The lodge is next to Wallowa Lake State Park with picnicking and camping, children's play area, nature trails, and a marina and launching ramp. There are boats and motors for rent, also waterbikes, water sports equipment and canoes. There's good fishing in the lake for rainbow trout and kokanee (landlocked sockeye salmon), from bank or boat. Licenses are available at the camp store across from the lodge. The cooks at the lodge will be glad to cook your catch for you.

Wallowa Lake is a jumping-off place for exploration of the 216,000-acre Eagle Cap Wilderness, one of the Northwest's more remote and unspoiled alpine areas, where rugged peaks reach 10,000 feet and there are more than 50 lakes, many abundantly stocked. There's an excellent trail system. All kinds of trips are possible, on your own or guided, on foot or horseback. Get in touch with Eagle Cap Pack Station (P.O. Box 416, Joseph, Oregon 97846) for: guided horseback tours, from an hour to a week; guided hunts, fishing and camera tours; as well as tours to Hell's Canyon.

If you want to fish farther afield than Wallowa Lake, try the Wallowa or Grande Ronde rivers, where enough steelhead and salmon come to make things interesting. If you pack into the lakes in the

Wallowa Mountains you will find rainbow and eastern brook trout in plenty, though not large. Lakes above 5,000 feet are open year-round but snow free only from June to August. Check with the Oregon Game Commission, Box 226, La Grande, Oregon, for regulations and advice.

Less strenuous activities include a 15-minute gondola ride to the summit of 8,200-foot Mt. Howard. There's an easy one-hour loop trail around the mountaintop, through wildflower-sprinkled meadows and with views of the jagged Wallowa Mountains, peaceful Wallowa Valley, Imnaha Canyon, and way off, Idaho's 7 Devils Mountains punctuating the skyline. Your walk may give you a glimpse of deer, maybe elk and bear. The Lichen restaurant on the summit serves lunch and snacks.

Or you could drive to Hell's Canyon, about 30 miles due east but 125 miles round trip by road—the last lap of which is steep, narrow and gravel. This takes you to Hat Point Lookout, where you have a breathtaking view of the deepest chasm in North America.

Wallowa Lake has historic as well as scenic interest. It is not far from the Oregon Trail, bits of which may still be recognized, especially if you have a good imagination. And this is Nez Perce country, site of the last great Indian war in the nation's westward push. The tribe's homeland in the Wallowa Valley was point of origin for young Chief Joseph's amazing thousand-mile running battle with the United States Army. Old Chief Joseph's grave and monument are at the north end of Wallowa Lake.

WALLOWA LAKE LODGE, Joseph, Oregon 97846. Telephone: (503) 432-4082 or 432-2484. Accommodations: twin and double beds; some baths in lodge with tub, some with shower, rooms without private bath have wash basins, baths in cabins have shower only; no telephones; no television. Rates: $12 single to $28 suite in lodge, $14-$28 in cabins; no meals included. Meal Service: breakfast and dinner; full bar service. Children welcome. Pets not encouraged (extra charge). No credit cards. Lodge open June 10 to September 10; cabins, May 1 to November 1 (weather permitting).

Getting There: By car, from Portland, Highway 80N to LaGrande, 82 to Enterprise, then take road south to Joseph and Wallowa Lake (15 miles from Enterprise). By bus, daily service from La Grande. By air, nearest commercial airport, Pendleton (130 miles west); bus service from Pendleton. Private planes may land at Joseph airfield.

SHANIKO HOTEL
Shaniko

If you're a collector of the offbeat and the unexpected, and fond of searching out little-known lore of the American West a bit off the well-trod tourist track, Shaniko could be just your dish.

When the first settlers came this was the land of roaming tribes, including the Ki-gal-twal-la and Dog River bands. Shaniko (Shá-ni-ko) was the Indians' version of Scherneckau, the name of the German immigrant who presided peacefully over a trading post and store here before all the excitement started. Though Shaniko is a ghost town today, in 1905 it was a rip-roaring little city at the end of the new railway from the Columbia River to the high plateaus of north central Oregon. Briefly the wool-shipping capital of the world, it was also the hub of pack-train travel to and from the goldfields, and smack in the middle of the early range wars between cattlemen and sheepmen.

The first permanent building was a saloon. Shortly there were 13. They say there was no cemetery because nobody died a natural death; those killed by gunfire were left for the coyotes. "Shaniko?" reminisces a survivor. "Sure I remember Shaniko! Believe me, it was a wild and woolly country—heat, cold, wind, whiskey and wild men."

As ghost towns go, it's lively enough today, what with the annual "Old Shaniko Days" and the Branding Dance right in town, and such Indian events as the Huckleberry Festival in the vicinity (at Kah-nee-ta).

Center of attraction is still the 75-year-old Shaniko Hotel—once called the Columbia Southern, "Queen of the Highland Hostelries." The queen may be showing her years, but she still reigns. And there's talk of designation as a State Historical Site.

The rooms, indeed the whole hotel, are really the way they always have been, the result of growing old naturally, not restoration. Hence floors tend to creak and one of the doors still has a bullet hole in it. But Sue Morelli keeps everything neat and in good running order. And you can forgive a lot of aging in a place where a wooden Indian greets you at the door and a mounted moosehead benignly supervises your signing in at the registration desk. There are no private baths in the hotel, but all three units in the next-door motel-type annex have private bath.

When you stop there, don't be surprised at some of the permanent guests. The hotel also serves as foster home to a group of oldsters who have been wards of the state for most of their lives. But there's plenty

Shaniko Hotel

of room for all in the rambling two-story brick structure. You'll take pleasure in the good home cooking, with fresh-baked bread and pies, served in the Home-style Cafe with a counter on one side and a huge old backbar on the other. And you'll smile at, but heed, the sign in the hall: "Want a bath? Make it snappy! If no one waits, we'll all be happy!"

Sue Morelli, who with her husband bought the Shaniko in 1954, is a fount of old-time tales and up-to-date enthusiasm. She'll tell you about the antiques, old photos and mementoes that crowd the hotel, and direct you to the local sights. These include the Wagon Yard, a museum (admission free) of freight wagons and stagecoaches that once clattered through the town, assembled over the years by the late Joe Morelli and his friend Ed Martin. Morelli, a former rodeo cowboy, was the instigator and hardest worker at the restoration of the old town and its artifacts.

In town, besides the museums and the hotel, are a clutch of weathered, photogenic buildings, including: the schoolhouse with its odd belltower, the 1900 jailhouse, the long, once-bustling wool ware-house, and the leaning but impressive water tower.

Shaniko is only nine miles from Antelope, world-famous rock-hound area (rich in agates). There's an annual Rockhound Festival at Madras 37 miles away. And the inn is next to The John Day Fossil Beds and what many outdoor people consider some of the West's most rewarding scenery—the high, wild desert country of central Oregon.

SHANIKO HOTEL, Shaniko, Oregon 97057. Telephone: (503) 475-3773. Accommodations: twin and double beds; community baths with tub in hotel, private bath with tub in annex; no telephones; television in lobby only. Rates: from $4 single, $7 double, $7-$10 annex rooms with private bath; no meals included. Meal Service: breakfast, lunch and dinner family-style; closed Monday and Tuesday in winter. Children welcome. Pets allowed but no barking dogs. No credit cards. Open all year.

Getting There: By car, east from Portland on Highway 80 past The Dalles, south on 97 for 58 miles. By bus, Greyhound from The Dalles. By train, nearest station is Madras (37 miles). By air, nearest airport is Redmond (63 miles).

TIMBERLINE LODGE
Government Camp

Massive Timberline Lodge, 6,000 feet up the south slope of Mt. Hood, evokes the rebounding spirit which pulled the country through and out of the Depression of the thirties. Built as a Works Progress Administration project in 1935 and dedicated by FDR in 1937, Timberline is constructed entirely of native Oregon materials and emanates strength and security.

Four hundred tons of stone went into the 96-foot-tall central fireplace. The hexagonal pillars supporting the great beams in the main lobby are Ponderosa pines hand-hewn to a diameter of six feet. But don't get the idea that Timberline is merely big. It is also a beautiful, liveable gallery of craftsmanship and artistry, devoted to three themes: pioneer motifs, American Indian motifs and native Oregon wildlife and plant life. Fine examples are found throughout the lodge: carvings depicting native animals and pioneer history; handwoven rugs (some made of rags and scraps from old CCC uniforms); marquetry; metalwork; paintings; newel posts carved from telephone poles. An informative leaflet leads you through a self-guided tour of all these wonders.

Mt. Hood is reported to be the second most climbed snow-capped peak in the world (after Fujiyama). Timberline is a natural starting point for hikes of any length. Only experienced mountain climbers should try for the top without a guide. For those who would rather slide than tread, the lodge offers complete lift facilities for the year-round skiing the location offers. Snowcats will take skiers and sightseers to the 9,500-foot level of the mountain. From there skiers can start the longest ski run in the country—eight miles down to Government Camp, another popular ski center on Mt. Hood's slopes.

Timberline's central "head-house" has three levels. The first-floor lobby is primarily used by skiers during the winter season. Off to its side is the Ski Grill, which serves informal meals. And around the corner from that is the Blue Ox Bar with its famous Paul Bunyan murals in glass.

The second floor has a comfortable lobby and the Cascadian Dining Room, with a fine range of choices for all meals, including such dinner entrées as lamb, sole, veal and salmon. Several enormous fireplaces warm the first and second floor lobbies.

The balcony on the third level houses the hospitable Ramshead

Bar, which has live entertainment on weekends. From large windows on either side of the bar you'll get magnificent views, either of the full scale of the mountain or, to the south, the high plateau stretching off from Trillium Lake to Mt. Jefferson, 43 miles away.

The rooms, which lie in the two wings leading out from the head-house, are comfortable and all provide spectacular views. Once you've been waked in the morning by the sun and gazed down through a clear sky to a blanket of fog covering the plateau, with only Mt. Jefferson and a few higher foothills peeking through, you'll never forget it. The rooms' interiors are pleasant to contemplate, too. Four of them, including the Roosevelt Room with historic mementoes, have fireplaces And in all, as the original furnishings and textiles have become worn, the lodge has maintained a steady replacement program. A dedicated group, Friends of Timberline, labors to recreate the handmade rugs and bedspreads and wall hangings and even iron and wood chairs and bedsteads. Timberline is determined to preserve its unique past.

A good way to start a day here is with a long, bountiful breakfast in the Cascadian Dining Room, while you try to absorb the splendor of the surroundings, inside and out. Further possibilities are many and varied; there are beautiful hiking trails, and if you get all the way to the top of Mt. Hood, you're likely to see smoke from the crater of this 11,245-foot dormant volcano. The skiing either at Timberline or other lift areas around Government Camp includes cross-country. You may tour the lodge for close-up marveling at the architecture and artisanship, swim in the outdoor heated pool (often open till late at night), play ping-pong, take advantage of the sauna, souvenir shops—or do nothing at all.

TIMBERLINE LODGE, Government Camp, Oregon 97028. Telephone: (503) 272-3311. Accommodations: twin, double and queen-size beds; private baths with tub and shower or shower only; some rooms with fireplaces; telephones; some televisions. Rates: $18.50-$33 single, $30-$50 double, $6 for each extra person; no meals included. Meal Service: breakfast, lunch and dinner; full bar service. Children welcome. No pets. Cards: BA, MC. Open all year.

Getting There: By car, from Portland, Highway 26 east, follow signs to Government Camp and Timberline (61 miles). From Hood River, 35 south, follow signs to Timberline (43 miles). Nearest airport: Portland.

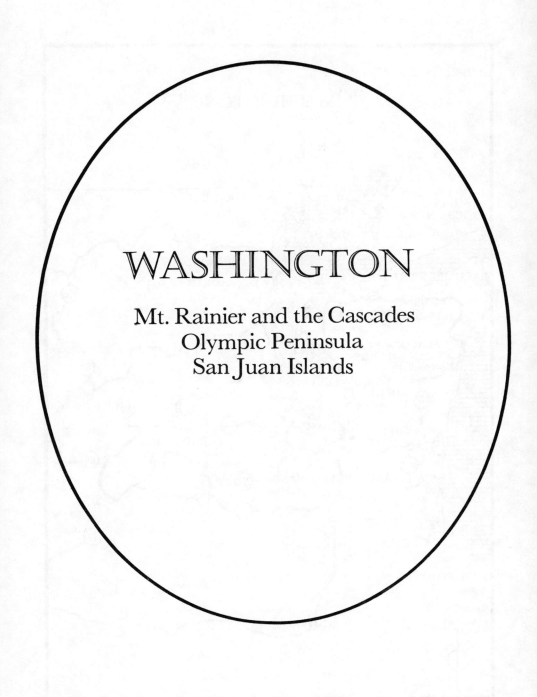

WASHINGTON

Mt. Rainier and the Cascades
Olympic Peninsula
San Juan Islands

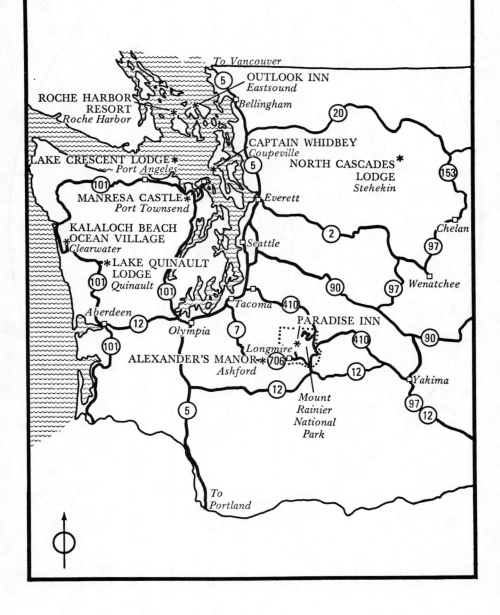

WASHINGTON

To Vancouver

OUTLOOK INN
Eastsound

ROCHE HARBOR
RESORT
Roche Harbor

Bellingham

CAPTAIN WHIDBEY
Coupeville

NORTH CASCADES
LODGE
Stehekin

LAKE CRESCENT LODGE
Port Angeles

MANRESA CASTLE *
Port Townsend

Everett

Chelan

KALALOCH BEACH
OCEAN VILLAGE
Clearwater

Seattle

* LAKE QUINAULT
LODGE
Quinault

Wenatchee

Aberdeen

Tacoma

PARADISE INN

Olympia

Longmire
*

ALEXANDER'S MANOR *
Ashford

Yakima

Mount
Rainier
National
Park

To
Portland

MT. RAINIER

Mt. Rainier is the number one scenic attraction in the Pacific Northwest. At 14,410 feet, it is the fifth-highest peak in coterminous United States and has the most glaciers festooning its slopes—26. Winter snowpack at elevations you can reach by car may exceed 30 feet. A young mountain, it was formed by successive volcanic eruptions less than one million years ago. It dominates the landscape within a 100-mile radius.

So much for the textbook superlatives. How to see Mt. Rainier best? We recommend an approach from the southwest, which permits the traveler to establish a base camp near or at the Longmire park entrance. Within the park there are overnight accommodations (summer only) at Longmire and Paradise, none at the other visitor center, Sunrise. Complete information is available at park headquarters at Ashford on facilities and recreational opportunities. The latter include climbing and hiking to some altitudes within and near the park practically year-round; skiing at Paradise from December to April.

Climbing: Everest conquerors practice regularly on this mountain. If you're an experienced mountaineer go on your own (but not alone) to the top, but be sure to schedule the climb with Paradise rangers. If you're more of a novice, climbing schools and guided climbs may be arranged, and equipment rented. Get information from Rainier Mountaineering, Inc. at Paradise, or write them at 201 St. Helens, Tacoma, Washington 98402.

Skiing: Ski tows operate at Paradise from December through April and the snow supply is usually better than at other Northwest ski areas, though facilities are not so complete. Cross-country skiing is good but one must be alert to avalanche danger; be sure to check with rangers for routes and conditions.

Hiking: There are 300 miles of trails in the park. Possible hikes range from easy one day or less walks from the road or from visitor centers to nearby eminences or waterfalls, to two-week backpack trips all around the mountain. Guides and maps are available at visitor centers. Register at trailheads.

For picnic supplies, minimum groceries are for sale at stores at Longmire and Sunrise (not Paradise) in summer. Nearest stores outside the park are at Ashford and Greenwater.

Horseback riding is permitted on some trails but check with headquarters at Ashford or with rangers in advance. They can suggest where rental horses are available (there are none in the park).

Fishing: You may expect good luck with rainbow, Dolly Varden and other trout. No license is required within the park. The stream fishing season is late May to October 31, lake fishing July 4 to October 31. Check with rangers for detailed regulations.

For more information on the park, write or call Government Services, Inc., 4820 South Washington, Tacoma, Washington 98409; telephone (206) 475-6260.

Getting There: It is possible to start from Seattle and drive completely around Mt. Rainier in one day, with brief forays to Paradise and Sunrise, the visitor centers on the east which give you a spectacular view from the 6,400-foot level. And if this is all the time you have it's better than nothing. If you don't care to drive it yourself, Gray Line runs one-day coach tours from Seattle. An alternative is to take the Gray Line coach from Seattle one morning, stop off at Paradise overnight or longer, and pick up the tour bus later. Contact Gray Line Tours, 415 Seneca Street, Seattle, Washington 98101.

If you drive, from Seattle, take Interstate 5 south to Tacoma, then highways 7 and 706 to Longmire; or leave Interstate 5 at Auburn exit and take Highway 410 to Sunrise. From Yakima, Highway 12, then either 12 (to White Pass and access to south entrance) or 410 (to Chinook Pass and access to east entrance). All park roads except 706 to Paradise are closed in winter.

PARADISE INN
Mt. Rainier

Mt. Rainier's Paradise Inn has been sheltering mountain people for more than half a century. Like its counterpart, Timberline at Mt. Hood, it's almost as beloved as the snowcapped peak that towers over it.

Built in 1916 with wise forethought to the rough weather ahead, Paradise still greets the visitor with a reassuring sense of solid stability. At 5,400 feet, it gives you an unobstructed view of the massive mountain, and is well worth a visit, whether you're staying overnight or not. But remember, though the mountain is always there, Paradise Inn is open only in the summer.

The huge lobby, mecca for day-trippers as well as overnight guests, is impressive, with its sturdy wooden columns and beams, stone fireplace, authentic Indian rugs, and plenty of places to sit. That goes for the dining room, too, which can take care of 200 comfortably. The food is good, hearty and moderately priced. The menu usually includes seafood, roast beef, chicken and ham, as well as other choices.

There's a cocktail lounge, the Glacier Room—rather inappropriately named, in view of the warmth of its hospitality, but effectively reminding you that Mt. Rainier is world famous for its 26 glaciers. There's a souvenir shop, and even a mezzanine with card tables, a happy solution for rainy days which, frankly, must be expected occasionally in the Pacific Northwest.

Rooms are simply furnished, comfortable and expandable. The management will provide extra cots, and there are a number of suites— two rooms with connecting bath.

A short walk from the inn is the imposing new Visitor Center, which at first seemed out of keeping with the prevalent alpine-rustic architecture of most buildings in Mt. Rainier National Park, but is weathering into a suitable compatibility. Though the inn is open only from June to September, the Visitor Center's snack bar is open on weekends all winter, for skiers and other hardy visitors. Winter snowfalls may reach 25 or 30 feet, but the Park Service keeps roads plowed and open for weekend travelers.

There are miles and miles of hiking trails branching out from Paradise, and if you're short on time or energy, a network of asphalt-paved walks will get you close to the high mountain meadows and stunted Alpine firs. Wildflowers are at their most glorious in early

August. Later in August and through September, the huckleberry, vine maple and mountain ash turn red. Keep a sharp eye out for mountain goats on distant cliffs and ridges if you have a camera with a zoom lens. Even if you don't, photographic temptations are irresistible. Deer and bear may approach, looking for a handout—but remember it's unlawful and dangerous to feed or touch any wild animal.

You may also take a short hike to the Nisqually Glacier, a steeper, three-mile one to the ice caves, and if backpacking, join up with the famed Wonderland Trail that goes around the mountain.

PARADISE INN, Mt. Rainier, Washington. Telephone (seasonal): (206) 569-2291. For reservations: Paradise Inn, Mt. Rainier National Park Hospitality Service, Government Services, Inc., 4820 South Washington, Tacoma, Washington 98409. Telephone (year-round): (206) 475-6260. Accommodations: twin and double beds; most rooms with private bath with tub and/or shower; telephones; no television. Rates: from $20 single to $40 suite; no meals included. Meal Service: breakfast, lunch and dinner; full bar service. Children welcome. Pets allowed. Cards: BA, MC. Open from third week in June to September 5 (or Labor Day); Visitor Center open May 22 to October 3; snack bar open weekends balance of year.

ALEXANDER'S MANOR
Ashford

Alexander's Manor, on the road to Mt. Rainier, was built in 1912. And like many a truly grande dame, she makes no effort to hide her years. Restoration has hardly touched the white-frame hostelry, except for the addition of a dining room wing a few years ago, glass-enclosed and complete with fireplace and red-checked tablecloths. Entry and dining room furnishings and decor are old-fashioned and eclectic. Wooden dressers and oak sideboards hold china and linens for the dining room. An old icebox serves some mysterious purpose. A cross-cut saw and a gilt-framed mirror hang on the wall, along with framed photos of the original inn, early loggers and pioneers. Somehow a gift shop has been crammed into the small lobby.

It's in the dining room that the new young owners, Jerry and Vicki Harnish, have concentrated most of their efforts. First things first, say the Harnishes. As a result, they've made the inn once more, as

124

it was 65 years ago when Elizabeth Mesler was the cook, "The best place to eat on the whole Mountain Highway."

Elizabeth was the wife of Alexander Mesler, for whom the Harnishes renamed the inn. This flamboyant New Yorker made his way westward in the 19th century. In the 1890s he landed at Ashford, near what is now Mt. Rainier National Park. Here he built a lumber mill and opened an inn to feed and house the growing number of visitors to the mountain. After the Mesler family ownership ended the inn was the well-known Papajohn's for some 25 years, and the Harnishes bought it in 1973.

The menu served up by chef Jerry is a delight, wide-ranging and respectfully cooked. There are steaks, fish kebab with lobster, shrimp and scallops, hunter's-style veal, chicken curaçao, quiche Lorraine and that Northwest delicacy, geoduck; and the prices don't alarm. A trout pond behind the inn provides the ultimate in fresh fish. Desserts seem designed for famished cross-country skiers or mountain climbers (many of whom indeed make up the clientele). They include a "weighty" and sinfully delicious cheesecake, wild blackberry pie and a spectacular strawberry shortcake. Coffee is home-ground, right in the dining room, and kept warm on a vintage wood stove. There is no bar, but beer and good domestic table wines are available.

While you eat you may look out the window at a newly installed replica of Mesler's waterwheel, and across the road to a mini-museum of railroad logging engines.

As for accommodations, there are none yet for the public, but the owners hope to be all ready by 1978. There will be 13 rooms on the third floor, 11 of them quite small and sharing baths, two larger, with private baths. Rooms will be suitable for one or two persons. One wing will be heated, while the "economy" wing will not, catering to hardy climbers and hikers. There will also be one room with private bath in the tower. Tower? Yes, Alexander must have been a man of whim; he built an octagonal four-story tower at one corner of his inn, for no discernible reason except to give someone a very good view.

Vicki Harnish is already assembling antique furnishings for the bedrooms. Meantime the owners are glad to arrange accommodations and dinners for groups such as hikers and biking clubs who are willing to rough it a bit. What with cots and guests who bring their own sleeping bags, Alexander's can squeeze in 30 to 90 overnighters.

ALEXANDER'S MANOR, Ashford, Washington 98304. Telephone: (206) 569-2300.   Accommodations (1978): twin and double beds; private baths with shower, community baths with shower; no telephones; no television. Rates: $12-$20;   no meals included. Group accommodations available in winter, at rates to be negotiated, with meals included. Meal Service: lunch and dinner; no bar service. Children welcome. No pets. Cards: BA, MC. Open May 1 through October 15.

Getting There: From Tacoma, Highway 7 to Elbe, then 706 to Ashford. From Seattle, Interstate 5 to Tacoma, then as above; 55 miles from Tacoma, 85 miles from Seattle.

NORTH CASCADES LODGE
Stehekin

This isn't the easiest place to reach in Washington State. You either take the spectacular five-hour boat trip up Lake Chelan, or charter a float plane; there's no road access. Or, of course, you could hike in across any of several mountain passes. Once at the lodge, you're in Stehekin country—in one of the most beautiful and peaceful mountain valleys in all of America, surrounded by breathtaking scenery.

The North Cascades Lodge has been a National Park Service facility since 1972. But for years, until creation of the North Cascades National Park, it was the privately owned Stehekin Landing Lodge. Wisely, the Park Service hasn't changed it much. Focal point is still the boat landing, where the *Lady of the Lake* docks daily. (She and her predecessors have been bringing visitors uplake from Chelan since the 1890s.) The rustic dining room, with coffee shop at one end and outdoor terrace for snacks and sunning, is just up from the boat landing. Food is hearty and well cooked, planned for people who are working up big appetites, leaning toward steaks, spaghetti and chicken.

Single and multiple sleeping and housekeeping units are available, some in single cabins and others in the two-story alpine lodge buildings. Most can be stretched to accommodate large groups or families. All are strictly national-park-rustic, with native woods the dominant materials for construction and furniture. Beds have bright plaid spreads; there are plenty of extra warm, woolly blankets; and there's ample storage and floor space for bulky gear. Some units have a tiny balcony, just big enough to step out on and get another revivifying look at the blue, blue lake and its necklace of mountains.

The first thing you'll want to do is explore Stehekin Valley. Take the shuttle bus 23 miles up the bumpy dirt road that goes from the head of Lake Chelan along the rushing Stehekin River. The driver is nice about stopping so you can photograph a waterfall or a deer or maybe even a bobcat. The road ends at a remote alpine paradise—with camping and picnic sites, and trailhead for the stiff hike across Cascade Pass. The trip isn't all through wilderness; you'll see old-time farmsteads and orchards, and one of the oldest one-room schoolhouses in America.

Climb and hike. This country is the backpacker's dream. The famous Cascade Crest Trail cuts right across Stehekin Valley, and fine trails go up all the main side valleys. There are also shorter hikes from the lodge that you can do in a day or less, and guided nature walks. Package hiking tours are managed by the Courtneys of Stehekin, with pack animals carrying the heavy gear. They have horses for day rides, too, and will arrange extended horseback trips through the North Cascades Park.

Take a rubber-raft trip for a day on the Stehekin River (river conditions permitting). Or do your own boating from the lodge dock; boats and motors may be rented. Fish for four kinds of trout: rainbow, Eastern brook, cutthroat and Dolly Varden. You'll need a fishing license, available at the lodge. Swim, if you're hardy; Lake Chelan is always cold, even in summer.

In winter there's cross-country skiing. The Courtneys have good weekend and weekday ski packages from Seattle, and give lessons.

Take advantage of evening programs by the Park Service, and inspect the Pioneer Interpretive Farm. Or just sit in the sun and gawk at jagged snowcapped peaks, forest-clad slopes and blue lake water. This is the kind of place where you can do as much or as little as you like. For more information on the park, write National Park Service, Sedro Woolley, Washington 98284.

NORTH CASCADES LODGE, Stehekin, Washington 98852. Radio-phone: (509) 663-1521. Accommodations: twin and double beds, hide-a-beds, rollaways, cots available for large groups; private baths with tub and/or shower; no telephones; no television; kitchenettes. Rates: $27 single to $42 for large groups for sleeping rooms, $27 single to $45 for large housekeeping units, $6 for each extra person; no meals included. Meal Service: breakfast, lunch and dinner. Cards: BA, MC. Children welcome. No pets. Open all year.

Getting There: From Seattle take Highway 90 (Snoqualmie Pass) or 2 (Stevens Pass) to Wenatchee, then 97 to Chelan. Or take 20, the new North Cascades Highway to Chelan. All these routes are very rewarding scenically. At Chelan, park your car at boat dock. *Lady of the Lake* leaves 8:30 am, arrives Stehekin 12:45 pm summer and 12 noon winter. Boat runs daily May 15 through September 30; Monday, Wednesday, Friday and Sunday, rest of year; no Sunday service January 1 to February 15. By air, float plane service from Chelan via Chelan Airways, near Chelan City Park (ample parking).

128

LAKE QUINAULT LODGE
Quinault

First there were the Quinault Indians. Then there were the homesteaders of the 1880s, who packed in through the Olympics or paddled up the Quinault River. Then came the loggers. Then a lodge was built on the south shore of Lake Quinault to put up the visitors to this developing country.

That was the genesis of Lake Quinault Lodge, one of the two distinguished historic lakeside lodges in Washington's Olympic National Park. Forty miles due south of Lake Crescent Lodge, Quinault was built in 1926 on the site of the 1890 building, which burned in 1922.

Lake Quinault Lodge isn't actually inside the national park, but it is in the Olympic National Forest, and the park boundary is just across the lake. The lodge is, therefore, privately owned and operated and not within the purview of National Park Concessions. That may account for a number of features you might not expect in a rustic forest lodge—such as a sauna, bocce ball, a happy hour, and gas-log fires in the new "Fireside Annex" rooms. To say nothing of facilities for conventions and groups up to 100.

But in spite of its obviously successful efforts to keep up with changing tourist tastes, the lodge retains a high degree of cheery, comfortable prewar charm. The pleasant, spacious lobby invites leisure and fireside chatting. Wicker chairs and settees are grouped around the big brick fireplace, with its gleaming brass andirons, polished hearth and real logs. The view is across a sloping lawn to the lake, startlingly blue on a fine day but just as captivating when silvered by rain or mist. This is, after all, the edge of a rain forest, so expect an occasional shower or even downpour. That makes you more appreciative of the coziness inside. And the sun will soon be out.

The lodge has a renowned dining room specializing in local seafoods and superb views. The lounge-bar mixes memorabilia of the heroic logging days with antlered elk heads, stuffed fish and other sportsmen's trophies. Accommodations in the main lodge are simple and maintain the original decor of the building, with cedar-plank walls, hardwood floors, period furniture (even to the old-fashioned claw-footed bathtubs). In the new annex, rooms are downright luxurious, with wall-to-wall carpeting, big sofas, queen-size beds and full baths. Most of these have balconies with lakeside view.

The lodge has a heated, covered pool, a sauna, a putting green, ping-pong tables, croquet and a private beach. You can fish from the dock or from a rowboat on the lake, which has rainbow, Dolly Varden and cutthroat trout, and some silver and sockeye. (Note: you'll need a license from the Quinault Indian Tribe, since the lake is part of their reservation; prices vary for weekdays, weekends and on- and off-season.) Upriver from the lake there is fishing in winter for steelhead. The unique attraction at the lodge is the one and a quarter-hour cruise around the lake on the little sternwheeler, *Princess Quinault.*

Hiking trails into the park and the national forest take off almost from the lodge. Trailheads for others are a short drive away. People at the lodge will help you plot a course, and you'll get pointers from the Forest Service and Park Service illustrated talks, held regularly in the lodge recreation room. For example: there's a short loop trail to an exceptional grove of huge Douglas firs almost at the back door. There's a 10-mile drive, then a 15-minute walk, to the world's largest cedar, on the lake's north shore. At the other extreme, just 17 miles away by road is the Graves Creek campground, take-off point for a backpack trip up to high peaks and passes or right through the Olympics to the other side. And don't forget that three of the world's finest rain forests are within a few hours drive at most, and the Pacific Ocean beaches are only a half-hour away.

LAKE QUINAULT LODGE, P.O. Box 7, Quinault, Washington 98575. Telephone: (206) 288-2571. Accommodations: twin, double and queen-size beds; connecting baths in lodge, private baths with tubs and showers in annex; some fireplaces in annex; no telephones; no television. Rates: $21 single in lodge, $32 in annex with fireplace, $3 extra person, $1 crib, $3 pet fee; no meals included. Meal Service: breakfast, lunch and dinner; full bar service. Children welcome. Pets allowed. Credit cards: AE, BA, MC. Open all year.

Getting There: By car: 40 miles north of Aberdeen or 124 miles south of Port Angeles via scenic Highway 101, take Lake Quinault South Shore Recreation Area exit, follow lakeshore road 2 miles to lodge. By bus: daily service from Aberdeen, by Grays Harbor Transit. By seaplane: to floating docks on lake in front of lodge. Nearest commercial airport: Hoquiam.

Lake Quinault Lodge

KALALOCH BEACH OCEAN VILLAGE
Clearwater

At least two things are remarkable about Kalaloch. First, the site. Perched on a bluff, the weathered, shingled inn looks across the mouth of Kalaloch Creek and straight out to the blue Pacific. Some of the cabins are even closer to the bluff, with an unobstructed 180-degree view of driftwood-strewn beaches, breaking waves, the Kalaloch Rocks, and all that ocean.

The second distinction of this well-known inn, midway along the coast of Washington State's Olympic Peninsula, is that it's been in the same family since first built, more than 50 years ago. Charles Becker, grandfather of the present innkeepers, saw the potentialities for a resort here in the 1920s and, starting small, built it up to a lodge with gas station and several cabins by the 1930s. Then during World War II, when there was apprehension about possible Japanese attacks, Coast Guard patrollers of the beaches were quartered at Kalaloch. During that era, the lodge burned down. But since then the present owners, who operate the lodge as concessionaires of the National Park Service, have rebuilt it and also 10 new cabins.

In this "new" (1953) lodge, the lobby-lounge welcomes the visitor properly with a crackling fire in the stone fireplace. There are game tables, books and magazines, an organ—and of course the panoramic view. Beyond are the dining room and the lounge; like the whole lodge, open the year-around. The Indian motif is evident throughout, with justification; Washington's coast has been Indian country for centuries. Kalaloch may mean "lots of clams," "easy living," or "land of plenty." Take your pick. Typical items on the dinner menu are a shore dinner (a "potlatch feast") of fish and shellfish, Hood Canal oysters, top sirloin.

The 10 rooms in the lodge are not large, but cheerful and snug, especially during one of the roaring storms the Washington coast can provide. All have private bath, bright bedspreads, well-polished maple furniture and white curtains. Six have ocean view; four look across the highway to the dense fir forest. All the new cabins have ocean view; the dozen older cabins are smaller and not quite so close to the view. (The Beckers have recently added, at a discreet distance and almost hidden from the lodge by wind-bent trees, a two-story motel: Sea Crest House. Several units have sliding glass doors onto decks facing the ocean.

Kalaloch Beach Ocean Village

Paths to the long stretch of flat, sandy beach are at your doorstep. There's beachcombing for driftwood, agates, jasper, and Japanese glass floats (for the lucky few). Clam shovels may be rented at the store for digging razor clams at low tide when in season. You'll find many streams for fishing in the area (steelhead in winter, trout in spring), and in summer you may have a chance to dip ocean-run smelt.

Kalaloch is in the ocean strip of Olympic National Park, and within easy driving distance of the entrances to the Queets and Hoh rain forests—those world-famous natural areas, where there is close to 140 inches of annual rainfall. It's an eerie, unforgettable experience to walk through groves of centuries-old, moss-hung trees, in utter silence, as though in a green cathedral.

If you've never investigated the other wondrous attractions of the park, Kalaloch would be one of several good places to start. Whether you're drawn to hiking, mountain climbing, nature observation, horseback riding, camping, fishing, beachcombing or beach hiking, you're close to it here.

KALALOCH BEACH OCEAN VILLAGE, Route 1, Box 1100, Clearwater, Washington 98331. Telephone: (206) 962-2271. Accommodations: double beds; private baths with shower in lodge and some cabins, some cabins with community bath; kitchenettes or hot plates in cabins (no cooking or eating utensils provided); some with fireplaces; no telephones; no television. Rates: $14-$20 double in lodge, $8 to $44 cabins (accommodating up to 9 people); no meals included. Meal Service: breakfast, lunch and dinner; full bar service. Children welcome. Pets allowed in cabins only. No credit cards. Open all year.

Getting There: By car, take Highway 101 north from Aberdeen (70 miles) or south from Port Angeles (90 miles).

LAKE CRESCENT LODGE
Port Angeles

This is one of the oldest and loveliest places to stay on the Olympic Peninsula. Located on the east shore of deeply blue, glacier-cut Lake Crescent, it provides both lodge rooms and individual cottages along the shore, as well as a new motel addition.

Lake Crescent is an old-fashioned lodge, typical of many in our national parks. Its spacious lobby is centered on a log-burning stone fireplace. There is a glassed-in sun porch with a view of the lake, where Sunday services are held, and a wide veranda with rocking chairs. Yet the lodge is also a place for the young; surprisingly, the gracious lobby has a pool table at one end. The manicured lawns include tennis and badminton courts. There are rowboats for rent on the gravel beach, Beardsley and Crescenti trout (unique to this lake) and hundreds of miles of hiking trails at the back door.

Meals are served in the sunny dining room with views of the garden through big windows and fresh flowers and white cloths on the tables. The food is excellent. Specialties include salmon, steaks, Quilcene oysters, Dungeness crab louis. The college youth who wait tables are friendly and obliging.

Accommodations include beautiful, gracious rooms in the lodge, with polished wood floors and paneling, perhaps a grandmother-style little rocking chair and French-type windows opening on the lake view. Lodge rooms have basins only; there are two baths with tubs in the hall. The comfortable cottages on the lakeshore, all in a row, are beginning to show their age but are well maintained. Each has its own little front porch. They are one or two bedroom, four with fireplace, and all with private bath. The new motel addition has all possible creature comforts but less character. None of these accommodations are housekeeping, but there is one rustic cabin without view but with kitchen, which will take a family group up to seven.

From the lodge, it is a comfortable walk by well-kept trail to Marymere Falls in a rain forest setting, and a rugged hike for the ambitious to the top of Storm King Mountain, which looms over this portion of Lake Crescent (about three hours and uniformly steep, but a great view from the top). The nearby Ranger Station and trailhead is a starting point for backpacking into the Olympic National Park. There are also exhibits at the station describing regional geology and wildlife,

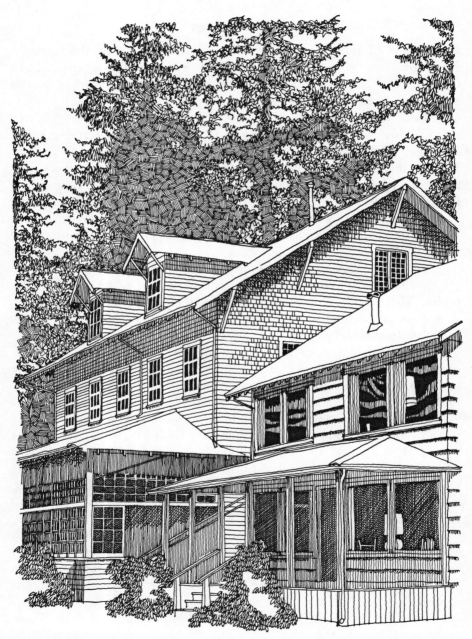

Lake Crescent Lodge

maps and guidebooks and advice, and a nature walk in the adjacent woods. Evening slide shows are given by the park staff at the lodge.

Lake Crescent Lodge is approximately 20 road miles from Port Angeles, where charter boats are available for salmon fishing and the Black Ball ferry leaves for Victoria. From Port Angeles it is only a short drive over an excellent road to 6,000-foot-high Hurricane Ridge, where the perpetually snowcapped Bailey Range—highest mountains in the Olympics—forms a backdrop for alpine meadows and grazing deer. Good walking trails lead you to closer views of wildflowers and snowfields and perhaps a mountain goat.

For day trips like this, the cooks at the inn will pack you a box lunch. Also, there is a lodge at Hurricane Ridge (open days only) that serves food and has interpretive exhibits and telescopes to give you a good close look at peaks and glaciers.

LAKE CRESCENT LODGE, National Park Concessions, Inc., Star Route 1, Port Angeles, Washington 98362. Telephone: (206) 928-3211. Accommodations: single and double beds; community bath in lodge, private baths with tubs or showers in cottages and motel rooms; one cottage with kitchenette, some with fireplaces; no telephones; no television. Rates: $10 single and $12 double in lodge, $13 single to $29 for cottages (accommodating up to five people), $22 to $26 motel rooms, $5 crib or rollaway bed; no meals included. Meal Service: breakfast, lunch and dinner; full bar service. Children welcome. Pets allowed in cottages only. Open Memorial Day through Labor Day.

Getting There: Located on Highway 101 20 miles west of Port Angeles or 137 miles north of Aberdeen on the scenic loop drive around the Olympic Peninsula, Lake Crescent Lodge is most easily reached by automobile. Port Angeles is served by Pearson Aircraft from Sea-Tac International Airport and by Greyhound Bus Lines from Seattle. Ground transportation can be arranged through Gray Lines in Port Angeles or by local taxi service.

MANRESA CASTLE
Port Townsend

It may have no portcullis, and you may spy a television antenna peeking out from behind a turret, but it's a very respectable castle all the same. It's a National Historic Site. And more important for the inn connoisseur, Manresa Castle is exquisitely appointed and surrounds the guest with old world taste and grace.

Manresa's history goes back to the end of the last century, its inspiration even earlier. Charles Eisenbeis, native of Prussia, came to Port Townsend to make his fortune in the late 1800s. Port Townsend was then just about the most active and promising city in the North-west, strategically located between the Strait of Juan de Fuca and Puget Sound, next to the timber wealth of the Olympic Peninsula. Practically every ship leaving or entering these waters stopped here. Eisenbeis started a brewery and a cracker factory and both prospered. He was the area's first big-time real estate promoter, and the town's first mayor. He built Manresa Castle for his young bride in 1892, in a style reminiscent of castles on the Rhine. Like them, Manresa is perched on an eminence, highest point in Port Townsend. For years it was the pride of the flourishing young town. After the Eisenbeis family gave it up it was acquired and occupied by the Order of Jesuits (hence the cross on the main tower). Finally in 1970, it was opened as a guest house. Since 1973, it has been owned, managed and renovated by Mr. and Mrs. Ronald Smith.

Mrs. Smith, in charge of restoration, has clearly brought as much discrimination to the task as did the original owner. On walking up the stone steps from the formal gardens you are greeted first with a fine Victorian drawing room on one side of the entrance hall and a small but charming dining room and the lounge on the other. The dining room impresses with its gold tablecloths, elegant lace curtains and enormous dark oak sideboard, but disarms with its tile fireplace, a quaint print of old Port Townsend over the mantel and a china cat on the hearth.

Rooms open off the long halls that run the length of both floors. They are neat and inviting, with fresh white curtains, very comfortable beds, period furniture such as oak dressers and gilt mirrors, and in most, an unbeatable view of town, Sound, shipping lanes and Cascades. Mrs. Smith's talent for discovering functional antiques is proven by each room's individual character. No two are alike.

Manresa Castle

Port Townsend, perhaps the most perfect Victorian town in the West, certainly so in Washington, is a natural location for a reproduction of a 19th-century European castle. There is an annual tour of the town's historic homes, but a few may be visited year-round. Several, like the castle, are National Historic Sites. The Smiths can advise you about what to look for. The town has a lively arts colony with summer seminars, performances and courses, and a growing number of art galleries, crafts shops, delis and taverns.

Besides culture, Port Townsend offers easy accessibility to the natural wonders of the Olympic Peninsula and Puget Sound country. It's only a 30-minute ferry ride from Whidbey Island, and 18 miles from Highway 101, which leads you westward through the "Banana Belt" of Sequim and on to the Olympic seashore and access to the National Park. Port Townsend itself has two marinas, seaside parks, golf courses and beachcombing.

The Smiths hope to start serving meals in winter soon, but you'd do well to call ahead to check. Meantime, a stay here gives you a marvelous excuse to dine at the Farmhouse, one of Washington's outstanding restaurants (weekends only). It is just outside Port Townsend on the Strait of Juan de Fuca, and its view is surpassed only by its sumptuous food. Reservations are essential; ask the Smiths for information on this and other restaurants in the neighborhood and downtown.

MANRESA CASTLE, Port Townsend, Washington 98368. Telephone: (206) 385-3398. Accommodations: double, queen-size and one king-size bed; most rooms with private bath with tub or shower, community baths with showers; electric heat; no telephones; no television. Rates: $19-$35 double, $27-$45 suites, continental breakfast included (served in rooms). Meal Service: dinner; full bar service. Children welcome. No pets. Cards: AE, BA, MC. Open all year for lodging, May through September for meals (banquets may be arranged at any time).

Getting There: From the Olympic Loop Highway (101), take Port Townsend exit from Discovery Bay. From Seattle or Tacoma, cross Hood Canal via floating bridge, take Port Townsend exit from 104. As you enter Port Townsend watch for signs to Manresa, one block north of Highway 20, on Sheridan Avenue. By ferry, take Keystone Ferry from Whidbey Island to downtown Port Townsend, taxi to castle. By bus, Greyhound from Seattle; bus stop about one block from castle.

THE CAPTAIN WHIDBEY
Coupeville

The Captain Whidbey, "the inn by the sea," is the kind of place that, after you discover it, you almost hope no one else will. Somehow, this venerable lodge on a cove on Whidbey Island's east shore has managed to preserve its character as an inn with the old-fashioned virtues: a warm welcome to families, comfortable lodgings, good food and drink, and most of all a genuine make-yourself-at-home atmosphere. This personality, obviously, was not manufactured overnight, but has grown over nearly three-quarters of a century, with management by the same family since 1962.

The madrona-log lodge looks much as it did when it was built as a summer resort in 1907, and when guests, coming by steamer from Seattle or Tacoma or elsewhere on Puget Sound, debarked at the private pier in front of the inn. The building has been in continuous use since then, though it lapsed from innhood into other functions three times, serving briefly as general store, post office and girls' school.

Today most visitors come by ferry and then by car; this aside, the charm is as it was. It starts with the huge fieldstone fireplace that greets you as you step through the front door into the living room, with its easy chairs and big low table covered with books and magazines.

Beyond the living room is the roomy dining room, with fireplace at one end and windows all along one wall. Here you have the best of both worlds: in the daytime, your view takes in the lawn, with a few picnic tables and benches under the trees and perhaps the ancient dog of the inn sunning himself; below the bluff, Penn Cove where an occasional ship or pleasure boat skims by; and stately Mt. Baker far off to the east. At night each table is a lamplit island in the firelit room. The food is good, too. The menu features native seafood such as salmon, crab, shrimp and oysters, as well as old-reliable "landfoods" like steak and roast beef. Children are kept in mind: The lunch menu includes a peanut butter and jam sandwich.

Next to the dining room is the Chart Room (cocktail lounge), brimming with nautical antiques and oddments: marine charts, of course, and club burgees from far places; a ship's propeller, an oar, and the flag of the Canton of Berne, Switzerland.

Up a winding staircase from the living room is the library, remembered fondly by many a visitor. Its shelves bulge with everything from classic Greek drama to Book-of-the-Month Club selections. It also has a television, and games for children and adults.

The nine guest rooms on this floor are not large, but quaint and comfortable. Beds, the only modern furnishings, are very good. Otherwise rooms are furnished with antiques, some dating from the inn's earliest days, such as marble-topped wash basins. There is one suite, the Honeymoon Suite, with bedroom and sitting room. All the lodge rooms share two baths but there never seems to be a traffic jam. All overlook Penn Cove, so you are lulled to sleep by the lapping of waves.

Other accommodations include four cozy cottages, nestled in the trees but with marine view. Three have kitchenettes and all have private baths and fireplaces. A step-up in the luxury scale is the 12 lagoon rooms in two recent additions, with verandas, private baths, many antique furnishings, and lovely views. They are not housekeeping.

The inn has recently added a gift shop where you may also buy wine and "take-aboard specialties"—a special biscuit mix, breads, jams, and cheese.

Small boats may tie up at the Captain Whidbey's own pier. There's clamming on the private beach (no season restrictions for hardshell clams here), also agate-hunting, and swimming in the lagoon. If you can tear yourself away from all this, all Whidbey Island abounds with historic and scenic sites to view. The island (second longest in the country) was discovered by Captain Vancouver nearly two centuries ago and named for one of his lieutenants. Vancouver called it "the finest country we have yet met with." Coupeville, only three miles from the inn, has one of the state's oldest churches (Methodist, 1853) and a fine little museum. Tennis units and a golf course are close by. Just across the narrow neck of land from the inn on the west side is Fort Casey, with its historic lighthouse and its World War II gun emplacements still in good condition. Around the point from Fort Casey is the Keystone Ferry which runs year-round (but only on weekends in winter—check schedules) between Whidbey Island and Port Townsend, one of the gateways to the Olympic Peninsula.

Don't miss Deception Pass between the north tip of Whidbey and Fidalgo Islands. It's a thrilling experience to stand on the high bridge while the tide runs swiftly through the narrow rockbound channel.

The whole island is still relatively rural and unspoiled. It's fine for bicycle touring. (Bikes may be rented through the inn.) Salmon fishing hereabouts is also a good pastime and can be sensational most of the year: humpback, Chinook, silver, king. You may moor your own boat at the inn dock and go out trolling, or charter a boat at Oak Harbor, seven miles away.

Harbor Airlines has package tours from Seattle for golfers, salmon fishermen, bicyclists and history enthusiasts. Write Harbor Airlines, P.O. Box 775, Oak Harbor, Washington 98277.

THE CAPTAIN WHIDBEY, Route 1, Box 32, Coupeville, Washington 98329. Telephone: (206) OR 8-4097. Accommodations: twin, double, twin double and queen-size beds; community baths with showers in lodge, private baths with tub/shower in cottages and lagoon rooms; some cottages with kitchenettes, all with fireplaces; no telephones; no television. Rates: $11-$16 single, $16-$20 double in lodge; $16-$24 cottages, $18-$22 lagoon rooms; no meals included. Meal Service: breakfast, lunch and dinner; full bar service. Children welcome. Cards: BA, MC. Open all year.

Getting There: By car, car ferry from Mukilteo to Columbia Beach, then Highway 525 past Coupeville to Penn Cove. Or, Highway 20 south from Anacortes through Oak Harbor, then seven miles on Penn Cove road. Or, car ferry from Port Townsend to Keystone east to Highway 525, north to Coupeville and as above. By boat, direct to Penn Cove. By air, daily commercial flights to Oak Harbor from Seattle (30 minutes) via Harbor Airlines.

ROCHE HARBOR RESORT
Roche Harbor

Accessible by land, air or sea, Roche Harbor Resort is a pocket of turn-of-the-century charm and hospitality at the north end of San Juan Island (second largest in the San Juan archipelago).

The resort is a self-sufficient complex: hotel, restaurant, cottages and moorage for 200 boats in one of the world's loveliest small-boat anchorages, and the most sheltered in the San Juans. There are also housekeeping cottages, a laundromat, gas pumps, grocery store and launching ramp. And, since this is a jumping-off place for waterborne travel into Canadian waters, Roche Harbor has a customs office.

The Hotel de Haro, still the center of activity, has been here since it was built in 1886 by John McMillin, pioneer business magnate.

HOTEL DE HARO

Roche Harbor Resort

McMillin carved out his private empire at Roche Harbor in the 1890s and presided over it until the 1930s. His company town was based on the exploitation of an extraordinarily rich limestone deposit. Lime was much in demand all up and down the West Coast, and for a while McMillin had a monopoly on the business in the West. He built a hotel (naming it for an 18th-century Spanish explorer) because he enjoyed showing off his barony and wanted a proper place to lodge his visitors. President Theodore Roosevelt was here in 1906, hence the Hotel de Haro's Presidential Suite. William Howard Taft was also a visitor.

The hotel was built around the Hudson's Bay post that had been on the site since 1845. Some of the post's massive original timbers can be seen, still holding it all together. The white-painted, cupola-crowned three-story building has a creaky but comfortable charm and has been scrupulously maintained. Most of the 22 rooms are small and simply furnished with period pieces, such as rocking chairs and washstands. The four suites are especially painstaking in their reproduction of the past. The Honeymoon Suite, for instance, has most of its original furnishings: a large walnut marble-topped dresser with ceiling-high mirror, cane-bottomed chairs and an oak settee, and an inviting double bed with fringed white spread. Wallpaper is an attractive floral pattern, and ruffled white curtains at the windows permit a glimpse of the ivy-twined veranda. The suites all have private bath, and the Presidential Suite also has a fireplace and private veranda.

Nearby, McMillin built his own house, now the Roche Harbor Restaurant. You approach from the dock, or stroll from the hotel through a beautifully groomed semi-formal garden. The restaurant's varied menu includes, as you would expect, excellent seafood from San Juan waters and beaches. There is a pleasant cocktail lounge with a lot of activity on a Saturday night when the yacht moorage is full up. The bountifully windowed dining room looks out on the boating activity and Speiden Channel. You have several other choices when hungry or thirsty: a doughnut shop in the hotel, a snack bar at the pool and (new in 1977) a poolside cocktail bar.

About a block from the hotel are nine housekeeping cottages, renovated from the company-town era, completely furnished and well suited to families who wish to stay awhile and explore the surroundings. Higher rates and six-day minimum stay, during July and August, apply to the cottages.

The resort complex offers an Olympic-size heated pool and tennis courts. Salmon fishing in the area is almost always rewarding, throughout the year, for one kind or another—Chinook, silver, king. Boston whalers and other boats and motors may be rented at the marina, for fishing or cruising. Clams are especially good and plentiful at this end of San Juan Island, as you may discover for yourself in the restaurant if you're too lazy to dig. (Check on seasons.) Rabbit hunting is a famous pastime on the island ever since the population explosion some years ago when a few bunnies were innocently introduced. There's no season, but be sure you're not trespassing. Farmers have become sensitive about nimrods who may aim at a rabbit and hit a cow.

There are guided trail rides, or horses to hire for those who wish to strike out on their own. Except for the grocery store at the marina, there are no shops at Roche Harbor, but Friday Harbor, down-island, has plenty: boutiques, an ice cream parlor, deli, gift shops, book stores, even a grocery that delivers. Guests who come by boat will find full services at the yacht anchorage.

Not within walking distance, but well worth the short drive, is the English Camp at Garrison Bay. This was headquarters for the English troops stationed on disputed San Juan Island during the largely amicable Pig War, 1860-1872. The garrison's blockhouse, commissary and barracks still stand, incorporating an excellent historical display.

ROCHE HARBOR RESORT, Roche Harbor, Washington 98250. Telephone: (206) 378-2155. Accommodations: twin, double and queen-size beds; four private full baths, community baths with tub or shower, private baths with tub or shower in housekeeping cottages; no telephones; no television. Rates: $18 single to $36.50 suite in hotel, $34-$40 cottages; no meals included. Meal Service: breakfast, lunch and dinner every day in season, on weekends only in winter; coffee shop; full bar service. Children welcome. Pets allowed. Cards: AE, BA, MC. Open mid-May through mid-October, weekends in winter.

Getting There: By car, take car ferry from Anacortes, Washington, or Sidney, British Columbia, to Friday Harbor on San Juan Island; thence, 11 miles by road to Roche Harbor. By boat, direct to Roche Harbor, or you may use docking facilities at Friday Harbor. By air, commercial flights daily to Friday Harbor from Bellingham and Seattle; at Roche Harbor, private and commercial charter planes can land.

OUTLOOK INN
Eastsound

One of the more blasé Seattle restaurant reviewers called this "a kinky little inn." The owners say they're trying to maintain a "warm home-like atmosphere reminiscent of yesteryear." An unbiased young visitor decided, after much thought, "I think I like this place." Somewhere in all this is the explanation of Outlook Inn's attraction.

But on one specific feature there's no doubt. The food. Strictly home cooking, with no shortcuts, obviously prepared by people who respect the freshness of a fish and the need for a soup to simmer for hours in a kettle. And the fresh home-baked bread! It's proudly billed as "prize-winning," and so it would be in anybody's contest. Same goes for the apple pie. Dinners include soup or salad, a small loaf of bread, entrée, dessert and Colombian coffee or your choice of teas.

The spot where you savor all this is a pleasant dining room with a view of East Sound and the cheering warmth of an open fire. This intimate, cozy dining room is, in turn, in a wood-frame, hundred-year-old inn. Outlook Inn, at Eastsound, is the oldest commercial establishment on Orcas Island. Orcas Island is the largest of the San Juan Islands. And the San Juans, as is well known, are among the most intriguing, remote yet accessible, getaway spots on the whole West Coast. So Outlook Inn is a very good place to be.

It was built, probably in 1838, as a hotel for produce and stock buyers who came to Orcas by steamer. (Trade in wool, dairy products and livestock from Orcas was the basis for the founding of Eastsound.) The inn has operated more or less continuously since, as dance hall, barber shop, pharmacy, jail, but mostly as an inn. An outstanding collection of antiques throughout the two-story structure bears witness to its roots in the past: brass bedsteads, marble-topped dressers, kerosene lamps. These furnishings, and the very gay wallpaper, make the rooms so interesting that you don't mind if they're not plush, and don't have private baths. Four rooms have a view of the sound and one has a balcony. But you don't come here for luxury—if you wanted that kind of thing, you would go to the resort hotel Rosario, down the sound a few miles.

What makes Outlook Inn unusual and maybe "kinky" is its ownership by the Louis Foundation, which purchased it in 1967 and has been restoring it ever since. It's the main source of income for this non-profit foundation, which has the hard-to-quarrel-with purpose of welcoming "people from all walks of life, from all religions, desirous of making the world a better place for mankind and, in turn, enriching their own lives." In an unaggressive way, the foundation is active in publications, education and study groups. Somehow Louis (he uses no last name) combines his role as a mystic and psychic with a superb mastery of innkeeping, and imparts to all the employees his dedication to pleasing the customers. The employees, incidentally, all donate their time to the foundation, and treat guests gently, considerately, efficiently.

Outlook Inn makes a fine little headquarters for your stay on Orcas. First off, it has its own private saltwater beach. Then in East-sound, at the heart of the island, you'll find a small historic museum, and several shops with curios, arts and crafts. It's just minutes by car from the island's justly famed Moran State Park, a 5,000-acre, mostly wild playground, with fishing, swimming and boating in two lakes; picnicking and camping; and even some mild mountain climbing. Mt. Constitution, at 2,400 feet the highest point in the islands, is easily reached by a good trail, and the view of the jewel-like archipelago and distant mountain ranges is worth every puff. Hiking and biking are popular activities all over the island. There's a golf course a couple of miles from Eastsound.

OUTLOOK INN, Eastsound, Washington. Telephone: (206) 376-2581. Accommodations: double and twin beds; no private baths, some rooms have washbowls, community baths with tub or shower; no telephones; no television. Rates: $11 single, $16 double; no meals included. Meal Service: breakfast, lunch and dinner; no bar service. Children welcome. No pets. Cards: BA, MC. Open all year.

Getting There: By car ferry, from Anacortes, Washington or Sidney, British Columbia, to Orcas, then eight miles by road to Outlook Inn, first building you come to in Eastsound. By air, daily commercial flights from Seattle-Tacoma Airport via San Juan Airlines; Orcas Air-port is a half mile from Eastsound. Charter flights from Anacortes via Harbor Air. By prior arrangement, the inn will pick up guests at ferry dock or airport. By bus, Island Empire Bus Lines to ferry dock at Anacortes, by ferry to Orcas, arrange for pickup by inn. By private boat, moorage at Standard Oil dock at Eastsound.

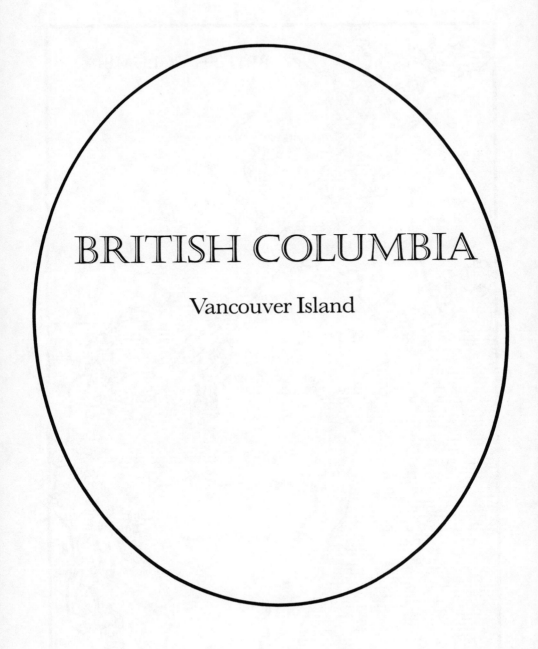

BRITISH COLUMBIA

Vancouver Island

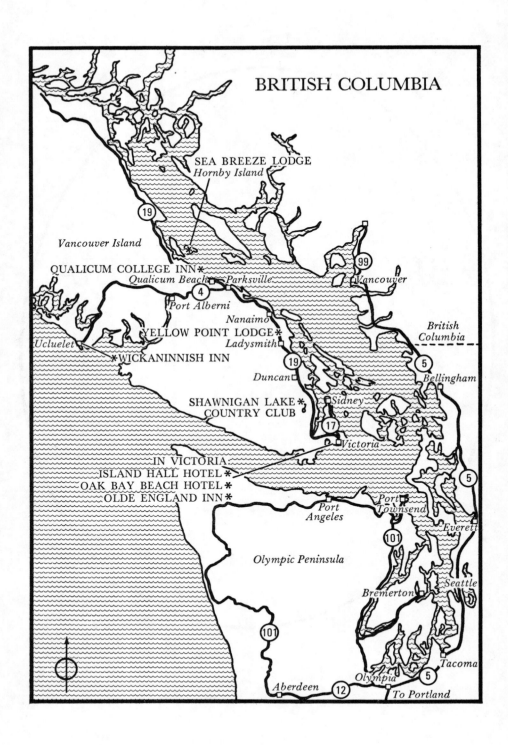

BRITISH COLUMBIA

SEA BREEZE LODGE
Hornby Island

19

Vancouver Island

QUALICUM COLLEGE INN *
Qualicum Beach □ *Parksville*

4

□ *Port Alberni*

Nanaimo

YELLOW POINT LODGE *
Ladysmith □

Ucluelet

* WICKANINNISH INN

19

Duncan □

SHAWNIGAN LAKE *
COUNTRY CLUB

99

□ *Vancouver*

British
Columbia

5

Bellingham

Sidney

17

□ *Victoria*

IN VICTORIA:
ISLAND HALL HOTEL *
OAK BAY BEACH HOTEL *
OLDE ENGLAND INN *

Port
Angeles

Port
Townsend

101

Olympic Peninsula

101

Aberdeen

12

Bremerton

Olympia

5

To Portland

5

Everett

Seattle

Tacoma

VICTORIA

British Columbia, of which Victoria is the provincial capital, joined the Dominion of Canada only in 1871, but a great deal of history is concentrated here. Not only the exciting adventures of exploring and settling a new land, but also the inherited traditions brought from the mother country. The result is as English a place as you'll find on this side of the Atlantic, with, still, a strong sense of the frontier.

Downtown Victoria is fairly compact and though there is a great deal to see, it is probably best to do your initial exploring on foot. Suppose you arrive by ferry at the Inner Harbour. At once stop to ask the polite, well-informed staff at the Tourist Bureau for maps and guides. Then off you go: to the stately Parliament Buildings, so like London's that you half expect to hear Big Ben. To the venerable Empress Hotel, where, even if you don't stop for tea (and if it's summer you won't want to brave the tourist throngs), a stroll through the splendid lobby is worth the trip. To Beacon Hill Park, containing the world's tallest totem pole, a deer park and a cricket field—a nice commentary on the melding of the Northwest Indian culture, never far off in this part of the country, and the English tradition.

In the other direction you'll find most of the shops Victoria is famous for. The temptations to take advantage of them will be irresistible, so it's well to have Christmas and birthday lists in mind when you come. Antiques, woollens, needlepoint, china, tartans, tea; and representing the indigenous culture, sealskin moccasins, baskets, carvings and Cowichan Indian sweaters. Partly for shopping and partly for a look at how things used to be you should visit Bastion Square, a careful restoration of a bit of old Victoria, less crassly commercial than some such projects. You'll find the excellent Maritime Museum here. By now you will have realized why this is called the City of Gardens; even on the busy downtown streets, hanging baskets of lobelia and geraniums delight the eye.

Under no circumstances should you skip the incomparable Provincial Museum, between Parliament and the Empress. There's nothing hoary or musty about this sparkling museum. It has the finest Northwest Indian collection anywhere, still being completed. Its natural history exhibits include a huge whale skeleton accompanied by that of a tiny shrew. But the highlight is the group of full-size reproductions of early British Columbia life: a whole street with its shops and lodgings (made realistic by the wafting of the odor of fresh bread near the bakery), a railroad station waiting room, a blacksmith shop. There is also a farmyard in winter and a startlingly moving mining scene, with the ghostly figures of the miners plying their gloomy trade at the bottom of the shaft.

Children love to stare at all this. It may be the adults who, exhausted, will have to occasionally seek an empty seat in the little theater that runs a nonstop show of old silent slapstick comedies. Moral: Don't try to do this museum in a couple of hours. Take at least a full day, two if you can.

Farther afield, and by car or bus, you will probably want to see world-famed Butchart Gardens, a 25-acre fairyland north of the city. Try to go before June or after Labor Day if you would avoid the crowds that swarm there in the summer; the gardens are still beautiful in spring and fall, even winter. This tour will take some walking (and standing to gaze) so be sure to wear comfortable shoes.

Getting There: By car, car ferry Black Ball from Port Angeles, Washington, to Victoria; Washington State Ferry from Anacortes, Washington, to Sidney, British Columbia (20 miles north of Victoria); BC Ferry from Tsawwassen to Swartz Bay (22 miles north of Victoria); CP Princess Marguerite from Seattle to Victoria (summer only). By air, daily commercial service from Seattle-Tacoma or from Vancouver to Victoria. By bus, Trailways from Seattle or Vancouver.

OAK BAY BEACH HOTEL
Victoria

Inns may come and inns may go, but Oak Bay Beach Hotel goes on forever. Despite the "hotel" in its name, it meets all criteria for a good country inn. Victoria's only seaside hotel, it is just far enough out of town to make you feel well away from the madding crowd.

The present owners, with due respect for a 50-year tradition of elegance, have adapted smoothly to the tastes of a more easy-going, less-formal clientele. Afternoon high tea is still served in the dignified main lounge, but nowadays one comes just for the pleasure of it, not to be seen by the "best people." Instead of an elaborate Sunday dinner, you now partake of a family smorgasbord buffet. The pomp and circumstance have given way to an emphasis on friendly relaxation, for families and groups.

As the management says, "We must establish a few traditions of our own." One of these is the taking of after-dinner coffee and liqueurs in the lobby, around the fireplace. The lobby is well supplied with groups of big, comfortable upholstered chairs and sofas and small tables for tea or cocktails. Soft light comes from brass table lamps, the six-foot-tall clock ticks gently, and there are always fresh flowers. For contemplation, there is a very interesting old "Crusader's Chair," carved with a fish and rope motif and an imposing lion on each arm.

Another tradition is a cup of cheer in the cozy Snug—modeled on the lounge of an English pub. Like much of the hotel interior, it repeats the half-timbered theme of the exterior. It has a fireplace, well-polished round tables, and ever so much atmosphere. It also offers good English pub fare: during the day, fish and chips, baron of beef, sandwiches and seafood; in the evening, corned beef or steak or triple-decker sandwiches. Plus, of course, beer and ale and complete bar service.

For more substantial meals, the dining room offers smorgasbord lunches Sunday through Friday, with an impressive array of 20 salads as well as meats and seafood. Dinner specialties (not smorgasbord-style) include, as you would expect, excellent prime ribs and Yorkshire pudding and lamb from Vancouver Island's own farms.

The Tudor-style hotel was built in 1931, after the original (1928) building burned. It is decorated in good taste throughout, and fine English antiques will greet you at every turn. The dining room, for instance, has two buffets dating from the 1600s. Rooms on the second

Oak Bay Beach Hotel

floor are large and comfortable, and include some suites of two or three rooms. But it is on the third floor where wonders have been wrought. The management has just completely renovated these bedrooms and suites and all now reflect different periods of English history. The Prince Albert Room, for example, all in gold (bedspread, drapes, valance), with wall-to-wall thick gold-green carpeting and a great dark man-sized oak dresser; and the regal King Henry VIII Suite, with its huge brass four-poster with lacy canopy (and a non-antique television set in the corner). Other period rooms include the Georgian Suite, the Samuel Pepys Room and the Elizabethan Room—12 in all, lavished with antiques acquired in England.

The scrupulously tended gardens which run from the terrace to the private beach, are right out of an English novel, and are a panoply of changing colors from spring until fall. There are sea views from the dining room, 17 of the guest rooms, and of course from the terrace and patio. You'll see passing fishing boats, freighters and yachts, to say nothing of killer whales, seals and ducks. You may even hope for a glimpse of Cadborosaurus, the legendary sea serpent of Cadboro Bay.

Though you will undoubtedly take advantage of your closeness to downtown Victoria, don't overlook the opportunities at and near Oak Bay. These include, for *very* light exercise, a walk through the gardens to the driftwood-strewn beach. You may enjoy a stroll in the neighborhood, one of the city's quiet, well-kept residential areas with lovely gardens. Across the street is a find for nature lovers and botanists: a neglected but interesting bit of fenced woodland, a preserve of native plants, trees and shrubs.

The hotel is a few minutes walk from the big Oak Bay Marina. The Victoria Golf Course is a block away, with fairways on the ocean. Beach Drive, which hugs the shore, will take you downtown in 10 or 15 minutes, depending on how often you slow down to look at the view.

OAK BAY BEACH HOTEL, 1175 Beach Drive, Victoria, British Columbia V8S 2N2. Telephone: (604) 598-4556. Accommodations: single, double, queen- and king-size beds; all rooms with private bath with tub/shower, some two-room suites with connecting bath; some rooms with balconies, some with sea view; telephones; televisions. Rates: $23-$40 single, $25-$63 double, morning coffee included. Meal Service: breakfast, lunch and dinner; full bar service. Children welcome. No pets. Cards: AE, BA, MC. Open all year.

OLDE ENGLAND INN
Victoria

As the name indicates, this inn is a bit of olde England transplanted to Victoria. Since Victoria, at the south end of Vancouver Island, is, in itself, the most English city in Canada, the setting is appropriate. Situated in a secluded wooded spot with vistas of the sea and mountains, the inn is within easy reach of town (five minutes by car or taxi, 15 by bus).

Built as a private mansion for a homesick Yorkshireman, T. H. Slater, by the noted Victoria architect Samuel McClure in 1909, it was acquired in 1946 by the present owner, Mrs. R. Lane, and her late husband, Squadron Leader S. Lane of Yorkshire, England. It opened as an inn in that year and remains a family business today with the assistance of daughter Dorothy and her husband.

After 30 years of devoted labor and research by the Lanes, the inn is now set in an English Village, complete with replicas of Shakespeare's birthplace and Anne Hathaway's cottage. There is also a conglomerate of small shops known as Chaucer Lane where reproductions of Harvard House, Garrick Inn and the Olde Curiosity Shop jostle purveyors of genuine English toffee, fine bone china and postcards.

Clearly, this is no place to come unless you are completely enamored of everything English. But if you are not put off by the tourist-attraction atmosphere and the crowds, you may find the Olde England Inn rather fun. You will certainly find it plush and convenient.

You have your choice of rooms in the main inn or behind the facade of the English Village. All rooms have private baths and television. Canopied and four-poster beds are prevalent, though not universal. The intricately carved oak four-poster with heavy silk canopy in the Elizabethan Room dates from the reign of the first Elizabeth. The King Edward VII Room is in Louis Quatorze style and has a graceful bed draped with purple velvet and the gold-gilt canopy from the bed where Edward VII slept in Warwick Castle. Gilt clocks, gleaming wall sconces and fine china vases and bowls add to the elegance. Fortunately, the management has equipped all the antique beds with modern mattresses. Seven rooms have fireplaces and one has a balcony.

Meals served in the antique-laden dining room include such items as roast baron of beef, Prince Philip's royal game soup, steak and kidney pyes (sic) and a "real English sherry trifle."

Olde England Inn

There is no bar as such, but drinks may be taken to or served at a rather large landing between the dining room and the first floor, where there are a few chairs and a few old firearms and a suit of armor to contemplate.

The inn is open all year, as are the village and other attractions. There are daily guided tours of Anne Hathaway's Thatched Cottage and Gardens. An Anglophile could easily spend a day immersed in the almost overpowering English atmosphere found here. The inn is a museum in itself, with an outstanding collection of lovingly gathered antiques: seven tons of them, the owners point out, "rare period pieces of furniture, china and a unique collection of antique guns, armour, swords, etc., brought out from England and shown to perfection in a 17th century Baronial Hall."

For the rest of the family there are public recreational facilities within easy walking distance, including tennis courts, swimming pool, a sports center with ice hockey and curling and a waterfront park.

OLDE ENGLAND INN, 429 Lampson Street, Victoria, British Columbia V9A 5Y9. Telephone: (604) 382-8311. Accommodations: double, single and twin single beds, many canopied; private baths with tub, shower or tub and shower; no telephones; television. Rates: $18-$45 single, double or twin, $30-$45 deluxe rooms and suites, $60 kings' rooms (with canopied beds originally used by European monarchy); no meals included. Meal Service: breakfast, lunch, tea and dinner; full bar service. Children welcome (babysitters available). Pets allowed. Cards: AE, BA. Open all year; winter rates (November 1 through March 1), second day half-price.

SHAWNIGAN LAKE COUNTRY CLUB
Shawnigan Lake

Old-timers who remember Shawnigan Lake the way it was way back when may deplore what has become of the area. But Shawnigan Lake Country Club is worth more than a nod to nostalgia.

Just before the worst of the Depression years, space for the original inn was hacked out of the woods surrounding beautiful, isolated Lake Shawnigan by F. C. Mason Hurley, a Victoria businessman who dreamed of an elegant English-style country retreat.

Hurley, working with local architect Douglas James, created a roomy timbered lodge 24 miles north of Victoria. All through the Depression and World War II years his inn at Shawnigan Lake enjoyed a peaceful, delightful existence catering to a leisure-minded clientele. But after the war Hurley's idea of an exclusive, comfortable get-away place in the country seemed anachronistic and he eventually sold it in the fifties. It has changed hands a number of times since then; the present owners purchased it in 1972. To do them credit, they have tried to retain some of the original flavor. Hurley's touch is still seen in the large, high-ceilinged lounge overlooking the lake, where he managed to achieve a feeling of intimacy even though the room is vast—a wide brick fireplace, deep comfortable chairs, old oak tables, a library.

Adjoining the main lounge is a billiard room, ping-pong tables, sun porch, television. On the lake side French doors open onto a long gallery overlooking the water, providing a lovely view that changes hourly, from the soft morning lake mists to brilliant sunsets, with the mountains and forests all around.

The original old stairs lead up to the dining room and bar, where the new owners have added an intriguing innovation. Once a month there is a special ethnic menu with authentic matching music: German, French, Italian and the like. The kitchen staff rises superbly to these occasions, and the meals are modestly priced. The chefs also cook up a special seafood spread one or two times a month, and in general try to adapt to the nature of the clientele at any given time; e.g., providing a plentiful supply of hamburgers and spaghetti when a lot of children are among the guests.

Again the old-timers will have to turn a blind eye on the surroundings. Forty years ago, the lodge's lake frontage had a peaceful, calm, child-safe swimming beach and mooring facilities for guests' boats. The bathing and the boating are still there, still peaceful and relaxing. You may take advantage of the inn's sailboats and receive sailing instruction, and there are rowboats and canoes. But new housing around the lake has made the water, sometimes, into a traffic jam (water skiers will need to be wary) and inevitably there are mutterings of pollution.

Rooms are available in the main lodge building, but beware of the one near the lounge, which with its banging disco-music can be a bit much on weekends. The others, farther down the hall and closed off by a corridor door, are quieter. All these rooms have been refurbished, with wood paneling, easy chairs and most with private bath. One has a fireplace. A few antiques are being gradually added.

Shawnigan Lake Country Club

Guests may feel more attuned to the inn's gracious past in the Robin Hood Annex, which is reached by a short passage under the charming old porte cochère. Rooms here, opening off a long hall, are much as they have been for 50 years: rather small, very tidy, with oak or white-painted old-fashioned bedsteads and dressers—very like your grandmother's guest room. Most have private bath.

There are also six cottages, about 50 yards from the lodge, similar in age and interiors to the Robin Hood Annex. In size they range from two-person to a large three-bedroom cottage that can put up eight.

This is a good place for active families. Besides water sports, the lodge has an indoor pool, saunas and exercise room, golf course and tennis courts. Although called a country club, the lodge is open to all.

SHAWNIGAN LAKE COUNTRY CLUB, P.O. Box 40, Shawnigan Lake, British Columbia V0R 2W0. Telephone: (604) 743-2312. Accommodations: twin, double and twin double beds; private baths with tub and shower or tub, community baths same; no telephones; no television. Rates: $12 single to $19.50 double; modified American plan rates available, with three meals per day plus afternoon tea for $12.50 (adults), $7.50 (children), plus room charge; special weekend package for two, September 15-June 15: meals, lodging and club facilities from Friday supper through Sunday afternoon tea, $88. Meal Service: breakfast, lunch, afternoon tea, dinner; full bar service. Children welcome. No pets (there are kennels two miles from lodge). No credit cards. Facilities for conventions, receptions, meetings. Open all year.

Getting There: By car, car ferry from Seattle or Port Angeles to Victoria, then 24 miles north on Highway 1, turn left on Shawnigan Lake Road and follow signs to Shawnigan Lake Country Club. Or ferry from Anacortes, Washington to Sidney, British Columbia, then ferry across Saanich Inlet from Brentwood to Mill Bay, then north on Highway 1 to left turn as above on Shawnigan Lake Road.

QUALICUM COLLEGE INN
Qualicum Beach

An exclusive boys' boarding school might seem an unlikely spot for an inn. But there it is, on the shores of Qualicum Bay—the Qualicum College Inn—a school from 1935 until 1970 and an inn ever since.

The owners have carefully kept most of the flavor of the boys' school. You see it everywhere: the Old Boys' Dining Room is the main restaurant; the Prefects' Lounge serves cocktails; the Headmasters' Lounge and the Masters' Common Room serve as banquet and convention facilities.

In doing away with the austerities required for a proper English boys' school—cold rooms, hard beds, rice-pudding-for-dessert, bare floors—the management has nevertheless retained the spirit and appearance so skillfully that a guest can imagine young feet pounding up the wide front staircase or shrill voices wafting from the rugger field. Pictures of old rugby teams, cricket sides and graduation classes cover the walls of the Old Boys' Dining Room.

The original building housing 40 students now accommodates only 20 guests, so rooms are much more commodious. A new annex has 30 additional rooms. All 50 rooms have bath and every room has a splendid view of either mountain or forest or sea. In both main inn and annex, rooms' decor combines comfortable modern beds and thick wall-to-wall carpeting with English inn-style furnishings: reproductions of substantial dark dressers and chests, cushioned window seats. Two of the rooms have fireplaces; one choice large room has a balcony.

Another theme has been added to the college atmosphere, and not at all incongruously: a mediaeval suggestion in the heavy, high-backed dining room armchairs, heraldry, carved bannisters. This theme reaches its climax at dinner in the Old Boys' Dining Room which features a five-course "Mediaeval Meal," with everything from manor house country soup, through a seafood platter and a squire's serving of open hearth-roasted chicken, to a harvest of fruit and a wooden board of cheeses. Many dishes are prepared right at tableside: the steak Diane and the scampi Grand Marnier are flambéed in front of you; a Caesar salad expertly tossed, brochettes served on a flaming sword. Luncheon offers such dishes as steak and kidney pie, the "Mediaeval Baron," "Junior Science sandwich."

Qualicum College Inn

The inn is approached by a narrow road through the woods from the highway, and could easily be missed. There is a sweeping curved drive to the entrance, swinging around the flagpole to the big oak doors. On the other side, the one facing the water, the beach-bound stroller is in for a pleasant surprise. From the inn the view is of a grassy field, a charming little gazebo, a wooded bluff and the water beyond. Reaching the bluff one finds spread out below a wide level grassy area that was the boys' cricket pitch, with its little white pavilion at one end. Beyond this there is another bluff, unseen from the inn, which does in fact descend to the water and a sandy beach.

Qualicum College Inn offers some irresistible package vacations, such as the Unwinder, a four-day opportunity to hike, stroll, golf, discover nearby Englishman River Falls, Cathedral Grove, or one of British Columbia's largest salmon hatcheries, swim, fish (boat and tackle included). The inn's kitchens will pack a wicker picnic basket for two loaded with old-fashioned goodies and a bottle of wine to take to the beach or wherever.

Other packages cater to fishermen, golfers, honeymooners, and a quite sensational treat for jazz addicts. Twice a year the inn hosts world famous jazz artists for a weekend restricted to 100 guests. It is expensive and the waiting lists are long (usually fully booked three months in advance), but it is worth it when you look at some of the legendary names who have been there: Oscar Peterson, George Shearing, Ramsey Lewis, Shelley Mann.

QUALICUM COLLEGE INN, Box 99, Qualicum Beach, British Columbia V0R 2T0. Telephone: (604) 752-9262. Accommodations: twin, double and queen-size beds; private baths with tub and shower; telephones; no television; conference facilities up to 100. Rates: from $14 single in winter, $18 in summer; from $18 double in winter, $22 in summer; $30-$40 for suite (one to six persons); no meals included. Meal Service: breakfast, lunch and dinner; full bar service. Children welcome. Pets allowed. Cards: AE, Chargex (BA). Open all year except for 10-day closing in January.

Getting There: By car, car ferry from Horseshoe Bay on mainland British Columbia to Nanaimo, 29 miles north on 19; or 92 miles from Victoria on 1 and 19.

YELLOW POINT LODGE
Ladysmith

What an ideal location for a resort, thought M. G. Hill when he first saw Yellow Point, back before World War I. This rocky point juts out into the Strait of Georgia, about 75 miles north of Victoria on Vancouver Island's east coast. Mr. Hill built a small lodge and cookhouse, then added cottages along the beach, and eventually opened the present, larger lodge in 1939. Now 85, he still lives in the old lodge, after retiring recently from active management.

A true country inn, Yellow Point Lodge is made of native logs and surrounded by nature with only slight modification by man. One may easily imagine arriving in a 1929 Pierce-Arrow touring car to enjoy a vacation in this serene, secluded setting. And a vacation or weekend here is still a chance to experience, if briefly, an otherwise vanished style of life. Here guests are encouraged to be self-motivated in their choice of recreation. And they like it. About 80 percent of the clientele are repeat guests of many years' standing—often reserving their accommodations a year or more in advance. One lady, now 76, has been coming from Wichita every year since the inn opened. The present managers, Mr. and Mrs. Bob Pederson, took over in 1976 after coming for nine years as guests.

Yellow Point is set in 180 acres of private parkland with more than one mile of beach. It sits on a massive outcrop of bedrock, leveled and smoothed by ancient glaciers to form naturally sculpted patios, more or less level around the lodge and sloping down to the beach. There are a few casually disposed benches and picnic tables, or you may sprawl on the sun-warmed rock itself. There's easy access to the 200-foot saltwater swimming pool, carved by nature out of the rock, and to walks through the woods and to the rustic cabins. From almost everywhere there is a magnificent panoramic view of sea, sky and shore line, backed by fir-clad hills and mountains.

The main lounge of the lodge is as relaxed as your own living room, with large stone fireplace, well-worn comfortable furniture, organ and piano, ping-pong table, games and cards. The 11 lodge rooms, most with private bath, are tucked into corners and under the eaves, adapting to the shape of the inn with its two peaked-roof wings. Room 5, for instance, has a tiny bath fitted in a niche in the corner and an outdoor balcony that looks through a giant oak tree toward the rockbound pool. Most rooms are rather small, simply but comfortably furnished with sturdy, old-fashioned chests and bedsteads.

Besides the main lodge accommodations there are 29 cottages scattered through the woods and along the shore. Biggest are the Parsonage and 3 Oaks, like family homes. The Parsonage has a living-sitting room complete with fireplace and homey furnishings, three bedrooms with wash basins, and one bathroom. 3 Oaks is similar, but has five bedrooms. Both have propane heaters. They are well away from the lodge, and are good choices for large congenial parties. Also, bedrooms in these cottages may be rented individually.

Then there are several smaller cottages with all creature comforts, oil heat and full bath. Finally, the Barracks—small cabins for two, actually sleeping rooms, more rustic and with wood stoves and without private bath. It's some hundred feet down the trail to the community shower.

Dining is informal, at long tables with a view of Mrs. Pederson's flourishing sun porch conservatory. Dinners for a typical weekend might be salmon on Friday night, roast beef and Yorkshire pudding on Saturday and turkey dinner on Sunday.

Besides swimming, fishing and walking, for the athletically inclined there are tennis, badminton and volleyball courts hidden among the trees. Tennis club members from Vancouver come regularly for a respite from their manicured big-city courts and deadly-serious games. There is also horseshoe pitching, canoeing and rowing—equipment available at the lodge. You may have driftwood fires on the beach.

YELLOW POINT LODGE, R.R. 1, Ladysmith, British Columbia V0R 2E0. Telephone: (604) 245-7422. Accommodations: twin and double beds; most in lodge with private bath with tub or shower, rooms without bath have wash basin, cottages have private bath with shower, barracks have community showers; no telephones; no television. Rates: American plan (includes accommodations, all meals, recreational facilities) per person for lodge rooms $30-$32 single, $23-$24 double; cottages and cabins $20-$30. Meal Service: breakfast, lunch and dinner; full bar service. No children under 15. No pets. No credit cards. Open mid-March to October, except by special arrangement for group meetings and seminars in winter.

Getting There: By car, car ferry from Port Angeles or Seattle, Washing-

167

ton, to Victoria, British Columbia, then north on 1 to Ladysmith, look for right turn with sign to Yellow Point. Or, car ferry from Horseshoe Bay, British Columbia, to Nanaimo, south on Island Highway three miles, turn left to Cedar and Yellow Point Road. By air, flights may be chartered from Vancouver to floats directly in front of lodge.

ISLAND HALL HOTEL
Parksville

If you don't mind the veneer of convention-attracting frills that so many good old establishments have lately felt it necessary to add, you may find Island Hall Hotel a perfectly wonderful place to be. In any case, it gives today's Vancouver Island visitor a reliably comfortable stopping point on the way north or west, and a convenient base from which to tour some of the island's most popular scenic areas.

Island Hall fronts on a pretty little bay on the island's east coast, about 20 miles north of Nanaimo. It's the oldest resort on Vancouver Island. When two energetic Englishwomen opened it in 1917, they hoped it would attract travelers on their way to Port Alberni or the north. It did. And some of the visitors from those early decades still pay annual visits. But there have been changes.

The first big change came in 1947 when the present owner, Mary Sutherland, and a partner bought the 24-room hotel, by then quite run-down. Largely on their own they renovated it and transformed it into an up-to-date, smoothly functioning hostelry.

The large, rambling, white clapboard hotel remains the major attraction to those with affection for tradition. There they still find the Golspie Dining Room serving such regional specialties as Nanoose Bay oysters and salmon steak, as well as old favorites such as steak and kidney pie and roast pork. There, too, is the Coffee Garden, an informal upstairs dining room for breakfast, lunch, dinner and snacks. The spacious lobby includes antique furnishings such as the sideboard from the former home of Canadian Pacific Railway magnate Lord Shaugnnessy, and Victorian writing desks, shelves of books, a piano and a fireplace. The intimate cocktail lounge decorated with a freize of tartans is called the Croft Room. The Scottish ancestry of Mrs. Sutherland (a remarkable lady, now in her 80s and still in daily touch with the running of the hotel) and her late husband is evident in the

Island Hall Hotel

naming of the rooms. Unfortunately, though, there is piped music in most of the public rooms.

The 29 guest rooms in the inn can claim no particular old-time character, but are fully equipped with modern comforts, from television to bed vibrators. About half have sea views. Several undistinguished but well-equipped annexes and bungalows have been built on land purchased by Mrs. Sutherland over the years, bringing total Island Hall rooms to 101 (most twin or double, all with private bath except for a few in the main hotel). The auxiliary buildings provide, besides lodging, four meeting rooms and two banquet rooms.

Right in front of the hotel is a thousand-foot private beach, gently sloping and ideal for children; there's also a children's playground. Recreational facilities for conventioneers and other guests include a sauna, Jacuzzi, indoor heated pool, tennis courts, shuffleboard, ping-pong, croquet and a putting green. Nearby are facilities for fishing, boat rentals, golf, horseback riding.

A big reason to stop at Island Hall is its proximity to such attractions as Englishman River Park and Little Qualicum Falls Park— both with impressive waterfalls, camping, picnicking and nature trails. Farther along Highway 4 is MacMillan Park with its magnificent stand of giant firs, Cathedral Grove. Island Hall is also a good jumping-off point for the west coast and the Pacific Rim National Park.

ISLAND HALL HOTEL, Box 340, Parksville, British Columbia V0R 2S0. Telephone: (604) 248-3225. Accommodations: twin and double beds (cots and cribs without extra charge); most rooms in hotel have private bath with tub and shower, all rooms in annex and the bungalows have private bath with tub or shower; telephones; television. Rates: $15-$25 single, $20-$32 double; no meals included. Meal Service: breakfast, lunch and dinner; full bar service. Children welcome. No pets. Cards: AE, Chargex (BA), MC. Open all year.

Getting There: By car, from Victoria, Highway 1, then Highway 19 (92 miles); from Vancouver, car ferry from Horseshoe Bay to Nanaimo (1 hour, 50 minutes), then north on Highway 19 (21 miles). From Tsawwassen (24 miles south of Vancouver), car ferry to Swartz Bay; drive to Brentwood Bay, ferry across Saanich Inlet to Mill Bay, drive north to Parksville as above. By train, E & N Railway from Victoria to Parksville. By bus, Island Coach Lines from Victoria to Parksville.

SEA BREEZE LODGE
Hornby Island

Hornby Island, a four-mile-square dot of land off the east coast of Vancouver Island, provides an astonishing mixture of old-fashioned homely charm and ancient wonder. Placid, quiet hedgerowed farmlands slumber cheek by jowl with fossil beaches, Indian petroglyphs and towering Douglas firs.

Sea Breeze Lodge, on the north shore of the island, was built in 1930 as a farmhouse, just one of the handful of comfortable homesteads that made up the population of the little island, but blessed with an enviable site: panoramic view of water and woods, private sandstone and pebbly beaches and tide pools down the bluff, where the sea is surprisingly warm.

The island has only a couple of commercial establishments, a restaurant near the ferry dock and the co-op grocery with its one gas pump. School for Hornby's 385 residents is only through the sixth grade. After that it's off by bus and ferry to Vancouver Island. Like all Hornby, Sea Breeze is very much a family place. Taking the children there is like treating them to an old-fashioned stay on a country farm, and they love it.

Sea Breeze remained a farmhouse until 1940 when it was opened to the public, with the addition of cabins and campsites. In 1972 it was bought by Brian and Gail Bishop, who have added other amenities for guests' comfort. But never, they say, will there be television, phones, noise, discos, bright lights. The one-story, dark-stained lodge still looks like an unpretentious private residence, and the family-style meals add to the friendly informality.

The Bishops cling to the old idea of innkeeping. All meals are included in the rates and are served in the main lodge's dining room. Menus combine farm style with sophistication: from Gail's fresh-baked bread to imaginative smorgasbord spreads. Local seafood is temptingly offered: barbecued salmon, butter clams, scallops and occasionally abalone. The oysters are superb. Salads come fresh from the Bishops' garden. Lunches are served on the patio. The lounge-bar has a welcoming fireplace, piano, library and card tables.

The eight rustic cottages can accommodate up to 35 persons. They're set rather haphazardly and quite far apart on the meadows around the lodge, and all have splendid views. Like the lodge, they don't pretend to be anything they're not: no king-size beds or lace curtains or precious antiques. They're little more than sleeping rooms, but well maintained and the beds are good. The Bishops correctly assume that guests will spend most of their waking hours outside. All but two of the cottages share a central bath and shower facility. The two with private bath (shower) are also housekeeping, but are rented as such only off-season.

The island is not without its oddities. To get to Sea Breeze you have to drive around an enormous Douglas fir in the middle of the road; the tree wouldn't move so they built the road on either side of it. Then there is a late-model car mounted upside down in the front yard of another farmhouse. The owner is said to consider it a piece of pop art. Maybe it says something about Hornby Island.

Guests have a wonderfully peaceful variety of activities to look forward to when staying at the Sea Breeze Lodge. Just walking around is rewarding. Walks on the beaches turn up fossils, Indian petroglyphs, odd rocks, and an incredible array of marine life. Walks inland are an adventure in flora and fauna and a delight for birdwatchers. There are ponies for the children to ride and tennis, ping-pong, boating, fishing.

SEA BREEZE LODGE, Hornby Island, British Columbia V0R IZ0. Telephone: (604) 335-2321. Accommodations: twin and double beds; two private baths with shower, community bath with showers; no telephones; no television. Rates: from $27.50 single ($182 per week), from $22.50 per person double ($147 per person per week), from $8 to $14 for children depending upon age; additional charge of $5 per day for cottages with plumbing; all meals included. Meal Service: breakfast, lunch and dinner; full bar service. Children welcome. Pets allowed. No credit cards. Open April 1 to September 30 (except for two housekeeping cottages which may be rented year-round).

Getting There: By car, car ferry from Horseshoe Bay to Nanaimo, then north on 19, 53 miles to Buckley Bay. Car ferry to Denman Island, drive across Denman and take car ferry to Hornby Island. Ferry schedules are synchronized to make this work, but do vary according to season and whether weekdays or weekends, so ask for schedules when making your reservations. Nearest airport is at Comox, 16 miles north. Nearest bus depot is at Courtenay, 14 miles north.

WICKANINNISH INN
Ucluelet

Though it may be closed in a few years, Wickaninnish Inn must be included here because it is a unique, once-in-a-lifetime kind of place. Built only in 1963, it soon became a cherished repeat-haven for wanderers who found it on Vancouver Island's west coast. They were especially possessive about it if they had come before the terrible 75-mile road across the island was improved. (It's fine now.)

What is its hold on the traveler? First, its very remoteness: a five-hour drive from Victoria. Then, it is right on the open Pacific, a world of whales, sea lions, storms, rocks and sand. The inn's weathered cedar walls seem a continuation of the storm-stacked driftwood from which they rise. Finally, the determination of owners Robin Fells and John Allan to give nature top billing.

Inside the inn, therefore, all is warmth and comfort but not show. The idea is to keep the interiors modest so the magnificence of the environment can best be appreciated. Bedrooms are modern standard hotel-style rooms, all but one with a view; 10, facing south, have sundecks with deck chairs. Most have private bath.

From the roomy lounge with its windowed walls you see the ocean and the whole wide beach. Count yourself lucky if a storm breaks while you're there to watch. As the management remarks, this will have a humbling effect. The lounge is unostentatiously comfortable, with fireplace, driftwood for decoration, lots of chairs and couches, books and magazines on the tables, and piano or guitar music.

The dining room (also with splendid views) is a little more stark, but makes up with its menu for any plainness of decor. You may count on superb fresh seafood—caught only hours before in Wickaninnish Bay. For example: curried Tofino shrimp or local salmon, barbecued as nearly like the Indian style as can be. And the West Coast chowder, crammed with clams and other seafood, may be the best from Alaska to Mexico. There are also non-seafood specialties, such as New York steak.

More than mere miles separate the inn from humdrum routine. The owners promise no radios, no television, no phones and no newspapers. And they refuse to organize any activities. Who needs organization, with the whole Pacific Rim Park outside the door?

This new park, incidentally, is the reason the inn may be closed, due to government policy regarding inns and hotels in Canadian parks.

173

So a word to the wise—go while you can. And reserve well in advance.

The weather is unpredictable, but can change suddenly from impossible to fine, so be prepared to go outdoors at a moment's notice. You may beachwalk, maybe the whole 16 miles along sandy smooth Long Beach to Tofino. You may study life in tide pools. Surfing is said to be exceptional here; the management will provide boards and wet-suits. Birdwatching is highly recommended and you're sure to see bald eagles, maybe a tufted puffin. In the dense forest behind the inn (there are trails) you may surprise a deer—or be surprised by a black bear who is likely to be quicker to run away than you are. Swimming in the ocean is only for the hardy; Kennedy Lake, a few miles inland, is better. There's fishing in surf or stream or lake. Nearby streams are said to abound with cutthroat for the fly fisherman. If you do well—or if you come back from the beach with clams, oysters or crabs—the chef will gladly cook your catch for you.

Wickaninnish (named for a 19th-century Nootka chief) is a good base for exploration of the Pacific Rim Park; there is an administration office at Ocean Terrace near the inn, where you can get maps, route recommendations and information on fishing and shellfish regulations.

WICKANINNISH INN, Box 250, Ucluelet, British Columbia V0R 3A0. Telephone: (604) 726-4244. Accommodations: twin and double beds; private baths with shower, community baths with tub and shower; no telephones; no television. Rates: $28-$35 single, $38-$45 double; no meals included. Meal Service: breakfast, lunch and dinner; box lunches available; full bar service. Children welcome. Pets allowed. Cards: Chargex (BA), MC. Open April 1 to October 31.

Getting There: By car, car ferry from Horseshoe Bay to Nanaimo, or Anacortes to Sidney, or Seattle or Port Angeles to Victoria; north on 19 to Parksville; west on 4 to Port Alberni; continue 75 miles to Pacific Rim Park; at Tofino-Ucluelet junction turn right, proceed three miles to Long Beach Road, follow it two miles to the inn on the beach. By air, scheduled flights to Tofino Airport. By bus, from Port Alberni to Ucluelet. By boat, M. V. *Lady Rose* (mail, passenger and cargo boat) sails, in season, from Port Alberni to Barkley Sound and Ucluelet. Check for schedules with Alberni Marine Transportation Ltd., P.O. Box 188, Port Alberni, British Columbia. Arrange in advance to be picked up by the inn at Tofino or Ucluelet, if coming by air, bus or boat.

Wickaninnish Inn

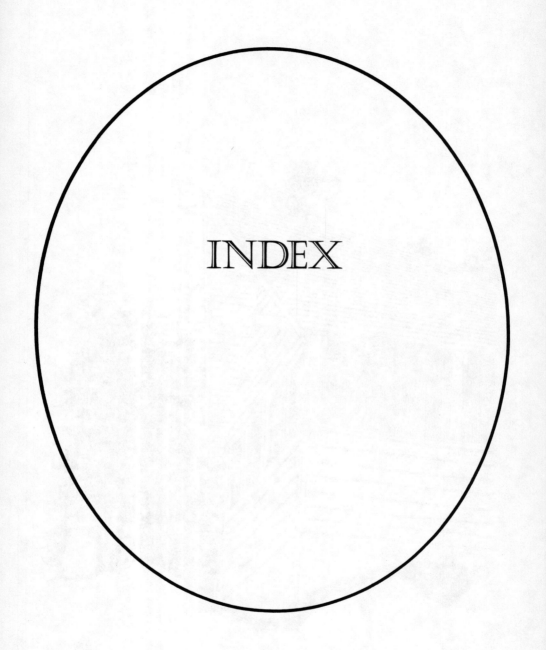

INDEX

177

BIOGRAPHICAL NOTES

Jacqueline Killeen and Charles Miller collaborate on the restaurant guide, *Best Restaurants of San Francisco and Northern California* and an award-winning monthly review of restaurants, *California Critic*. Ms. Killeen, a fourth-generation Californian, is also the author of *101 Nights in California* (a guide) and *101 Secrets of California Chefs* (a cookbook). Miller, also a native Californian, is the author of the travel guide, *Skiing Western America*.

Rachel Bard has a master's degree in history from the University of Washington and is presently working on a book on the Spanish-Basque province of Navarre. A native Washingtonian, teacher, and freelance writer, she is also the author of *Squash* (a cookbook). Ms. Bard's collaborators on writing and researching the inns of the Northwest are her cousin Peter Vogel, a civil engineer, and his wife Neva, a teacher.

Roy Killeen, whose drawings illustrate this book, is an architect, formerly with Anshen and Allen of San Francisco. He also has designed 101 Productions' "Mini-Mansion" series of historical architectural models and illustrated a number of other 101 books.

All of the contributors to *Country Inns of the Far West* share an avid interest in history, food and spending their rare leisure moments in country inns.